First World War
and Army of Occupation
War Diary
France, Belgium and Germany

63 (ROYAL NAVAL) DIVISION
189 Infantry Brigade
Drake Battalion
1 July 1916 - 30 April 1918

WO95/3114/1

The Naval & Military Press Ltd
www.nmarchive.com
Published in association with The National Archives

Published by

The Naval & Military Press Ltd

Unit 10 Ridgewood Industrial Park,

Uckfield, East Sussex,

TN22 5QE England

Tel: +44 (0) 1825 749494

www.naval-military-press.com

www.nmarchive.com

This diary has been reprinted in facsimile from the original. Any imperfections are inevitably reproduced and the quality may fall short of modern type and cartographic standards.

© Crown Copyright
Images reproduced by permission of The National Archives, London, England, 2015.

Contents

Document type	Place/Title	Date From	Date To
Heading	WO95/3114-1		
Heading	63rd (RN) Division 189th Infy Bde Drake Battalion Jly 1916 Apr 1919		
Heading	War Diary Drake Battn 189 Bde From July 1st 1916 To Aug 1916 Volume 2		
War Diary	Coupigny	01/07/1916	10/07/1916
War Diary	Trenches	13/07/1916	14/07/1916
War Diary	Verdrel	16/07/1916	16/07/1916
War Diary	Bovigny Boueffles	18/07/1916	18/07/1916
War Diary	Boueffles	19/07/1916	19/07/1916
War Diary	Ablains	19/07/1916	19/07/1916
War Diary	Nazaire	19/07/1916	19/07/1916
War Diary	Ablain	25/07/1916	25/07/1916
War Diary	Trenches Souchez 1 Sector	31/07/1916	01/08/1916
Miscellaneous	To Officer i/c A.G's Office Base.	01/09/1916	01/09/1916
War Diary	Ablain St Nazaire	01/08/1916	06/08/1916
War Diary	Souchez I Sector	07/08/1916	09/08/1916
War Diary	Souchez I Sector	10/08/1916	12/08/1916
War Diary	Ablain St. Nazaire	13/08/1916	14/08/1916
War Diary	Aix Noulette Wood	15/08/1916	19/08/1916
War Diary	Souchez I Sector	20/08/1916	25/08/1916
War Diary	Aix Noulette Wood	26/08/1916	31/08/1916
Miscellaneous	To Officer i/c A.G's Office Base.	01/10/1916	01/10/1916
War Diary	Souchez I Sector	01/09/1916	01/09/1916
War Diary	Lorette Sector	07/09/1916	07/09/1916
War Diary	Souchezi Sector	13/09/1916	18/09/1916
War Diary	Bouvigny Wood Huts	19/09/1916	20/09/1916
War Diary	Frevillers	21/09/1916	30/09/1916
Heading	War Diary of Drake Battalion From 1st Oct 1916 31st Oct1916		
War Diary	Frevillers	01/10/1916	04/10/1916
War Diary	Forceville	05/10/1916	08/10/1916
War Diary	Englebelmer	09/10/1916	16/10/1916
War Diary	Y Ravine Sector	17/10/1916	17/10/1916
War Diary	Englebelmer	18/10/1916	20/10/1916
War Diary	Mesnil	21/10/1916	23/10/1916
War Diary	Englebelmer	24/10/1916	26/10/1916
War Diary	Hamel Sector	27/10/1916	30/10/1916
War Diary	Headauville	31/10/1916	31/10/1916
Heading	War Diary Drake Bn From 1-11-16 To 30-11-16 Volume VI		
War Diary	Puichvillers	01/11/1916	05/11/1916
War Diary	Headauville	06/11/1916	06/11/1916
War Diary	Englebelmer	07/11/1916	12/11/1916
War Diary	In Front Of Hamel Sector	13/11/1916	15/11/1916
War Diary	Arqueves	16/11/1916	18/11/1916
War Diary	Doullens	19/11/1916	19/11/1916
War Diary	Candas	20/11/1916	21/11/1916
War Diary	Domqueur	22/11/1916	22/11/1916
War Diary	St Riquer	23/11/1916	23/11/1916

Type	Location	Start	End
War Diary	Hautvillers	24/11/1916	24/11/1916
War Diary	St.Quentin	25/11/1916	27/12/1916
War Diary	Le Crotoy	27/12/1916	31/12/1916
War Diary	Le Crotoy	01/01/1917	13/01/1917
War Diary	Hautvillers	13/01/1917	14/01/1917
War Diary	Noyelle	14/01/1917	15/01/1917
War Diary	Candas	15/01/1917	17/01/1917
War Diary	Rubempre	17/01/1917	18/01/1917
War Diary	Hamel	18/01/1917	18/01/1917
War Diary	In Front Of Beaucourt Sector	19/01/1917	27/01/1917
War Diary	Forceville	27/01/1917	31/01/1917
Heading	War Diary of Drake Battalion From 1st Febr 1917 To 28th Febr 1917		
War Diary	Forceville	01/02/1917	01/02/1917
War Diary	Beaucourt Rd Sub Sector	02/02/1917	03/02/1917
War Diary	Beaucourt Trench	03/02/1917	05/02/1917
War Diary	Old German Front Line	06/02/1917	10/02/1917
War Diary	Donnet's Post	10/02/1917	13/02/1917
War Diary	Thiepval Wood	14/02/1917	16/02/1917
War Diary	Old German Front Line	17/02/1917	19/02/1917
War Diary	Old German 3rd Line	20/02/1917	20/02/1917
War Diary	Old German 1st Line	21/02/1917	24/02/1917
War Diary	Beaucourt Caves	25/02/1917	25/02/1917
War Diary	Sunken Road	25/02/1917	26/02/1917
War Diary	Bruce Post	27/02/1917	28/02/1917
Operation(al) Order(s)	Drake Battalion Order No 5	03/02/1917	03/02/1917
Miscellaneous	Report on the Action of the Drake Battn in the Operations	03/02/1917	03/02/1917
War Diary	Spring Garden Camp S Of Ovillers	01/03/1917	18/03/1917
War Diary	Warloy	19/03/1917	19/03/1917
War Diary	Val de Maison	20/03/1917	20/03/1917
War Diary	Visee & Ransart	21/03/1917	21/03/1917
War Diary	Nuncq	22/03/1917	23/03/1917
War Diary	Bours	24/03/1917	24/03/1917
War Diary	Rely	25/03/1917	25/03/1917
War Diary	Vendin-Lez-Bethune	26/03/1917	03/04/1917
War Diary	Houchin	08/04/1917	10/04/1917
War Diary	Frevillers	11/04/1917	13/04/1917
War Diary	Ecoivres	13/04/1917	13/04/1917
War Diary	Pont-Du-Four	14/04/1917	20/04/1917
War Diary	Gavrelle Sec	21/04/1917	24/04/1917
War Diary	St.Catherine Maroeuil	25/04/1917	27/04/1917
War Diary	Frevillers	28/04/1917	28/04/1917
War Diary	Magnicourt	29/04/1917	30/04/1917
Operation(al) Order(s)	Drake Battalion Order No. 3		
Miscellaneous	189th Infantry Brigade No G 234		
Operation(al) Order(s)	Drake Battalion Order No 4		
War Diary	Magnicourt	01/05/1917	04/05/1917
War Diary	Roclincourt	04/05/1917	19/05/1917
War Diary	St Catherine	20/05/1917	01/06/1917
War Diary	See Ref Above	02/06/1917	04/06/1917
War Diary	Gavrelle	05/06/1917	11/06/1917
War Diary	Rochlincourt	12/06/1917	19/06/1917
War Diary	Mounil	21/06/1917	31/08/1917
Heading	War Diary Drake Battalion 189th Infantry Brigade From 1st September 1917 To 30th September 1917		

War Diary		01/09/1917	30/09/1917
War Diary	In The Fld Tinques	01/10/1917	02/10/1917
War Diary	Field	03/10/1917	11/10/1917
War Diary	In The Field	12/10/1917	19/10/1917
War Diary	Field	20/10/1917	30/11/1917
Operation(al) Order(s)	Drake Battalion Order No.	02/11/1917	02/11/1917
War Diary		01/12/1917	01/01/1918
War Diary	In The Field	01/01/1918	08/01/1918
War Diary	Metz	09/01/1918	22/02/1918
War Diary	Ribecourt	23/01/1918	28/01/1918
Heading	189th Brigade 63rd Division Drake Battalion March 1918		
War Diary	In The Field	01/03/1918	31/03/1918
Heading	War Diary Drake Battalion April 1918		
War Diary	In The Field	01/04/1918	30/04/1918
War Diary	Toutencourt	01/05/1918	08/05/1918
War Diary	Mesnil	08/05/1918	14/05/1918
War Diary	Forceville	14/05/1918	19/05/1918
War Diary	Englebelmer	20/05/1918	24/05/1918
War Diary	Mesnil	25/05/1918	01/06/1918
War Diary	Forceville	01/06/1918	03/06/1918
War Diary	Rubempre	04/06/1918	22/06/1918
War Diary	Auchonvillers	23/06/1918	30/06/1918
War Diary	Mailly Right Sector	01/07/1918	11/07/1918
War Diary	Auchonvillers	11/07/1918	31/07/1918
Heading	Cover For Documents. Nature Of Enclosures. Report on raid carried out by "Drake" Battalion on 12th/13th July 1918.		
Operation(al) Order(s)	63rd (RN) Division Order No. 247		
Miscellaneous	Reference 63rd (RN) Division Order No 247	12/07/1918	12/07/1918
Operation(al) Order(s)	Drake Battalion Operation Order No 21	08/07/1918	08/07/1918
Miscellaneous	Appendix No 1 To be read in conjunction with Operation Order No.21.		
Miscellaneous	Appendix No II. To be read in conjunction with Operation Order No.21.		
Miscellaneous	Appendix No III. To be read in conjunction with Operation Order No.21.		
Operation(al) Order(s)	63rd (RN) Divisional Artillery Operation Order No. 204	09/07/1918	09/07/1918
Miscellaneous	M G /1143	11/07/1918	11/07/1918
Operation(al) Order(s)	D Coy Drake Battalion Operation Order For Raid	10/07/1918	10/07/1918
Operation(al) Order(s)	63rd (RN) Machine Gun Battalion Operation Order No 42	13/07/1918	13/07/1918
Miscellaneous	Congratulatory Wires Reference Raid	14/07/1918	14/07/1918
Miscellaneous	63rd (RN) Division No. GA 5/19	15/07/1918	15/07/1918
Miscellaneous	189th Infantry Brigade B.M.1/484	14/07/1918	14/07/1918
Miscellaneous	V Corps G X 3908	20/07/1918	20/07/1918
Operation(al) Order(s)	189 Infantry Brigade Order No 29	10/07/1918	10/07/1918
Miscellaneous	189th Infantry Brigade	11/07/1918	11/07/1918
Miscellaneous	Table A		
Miscellaneous	Table B		
Miscellaneous	Table C		
Miscellaneous	Table D		
Miscellaneous	Table E		
Miscellaneous	Report Of Raid Carried Out By Drake Battalion		
Map	Map X		
Miscellaneous	Table A		

Miscellaneous	Table B		
Miscellaneous	Table C		
Miscellaneous	Appendix No II. To be read in conjunction with Operation Order No.21.		
Miscellaneous	Appendix No III. To be read in conjunction with Operation Order No.21.		
Miscellaneous	Appendix No I. To be read in conjunction with Operation Order No.21.		
Miscellaneous	Scheme For Raid		
Operation(al) Order(s)	Drake Battalion Operation Order No. 21	08/07/1918	08/07/1918
Operation(al) Order(s)	D Coy Drake Battalion Operation Order For Raid	10/07/1918	10/07/1918
Miscellaneous	Report On Raid Carried Out By Drake Battalion		
Map	Map Y		
Map	Map		
War Diary	Louvencourt	01/08/1918	03/08/1918
War Diary	Puchevillers	04/08/1918	07/08/1918
War Diary	Behencourt	09/08/1918	13/08/1918
War Diary	Sarton	14/08/1918	18/08/1918
War Diary	Vauchelles	18/08/1918	19/08/1918
War Diary	Souastre	19/08/1918	22/08/1918
War Diary	Bucquoy	23/08/1918	31/08/1918
War Diary	Boiry St Rictrude	01/09/1918	08/09/1918
War Diary	Barvy	09/09/1918	16/09/1918
War Diary	Ransart	17/09/1918	18/09/1918
War Diary	St Leger	19/09/1918	25/09/1918
War Diary	Pronville	26/09/1918	27/09/1918
War Diary	Mouevres	27/09/1918	30/11/1918
War Diary	Dour	01/12/1918	31/01/1919
War Diary	Dour Belgium	21/02/1919	21/02/1919
War Diary	Dour Belgium	01/03/1919	31/03/1919
War Diary	Dour Belgium	01/04/1918	30/04/1918

woof 3114(1)

woof 3114(1)

63RD (RN) DIVISION
189TH INFY BDE

DRAKE BATTALION
JLY 1916-APR 1919

To. 189th Brigade.
From H.Q. Drake Battⁿ. July–Aug 1st

CONFIDENTIAL

Headquarters Drake Battⁿ.
August 1st 1916.

WAR DIARY
of
DRAKE BATTⁿ 189th Bde
From
July 1st 1916.
To
Aug 1st 1916.

VOLUME 2.

To Headquarters
189th Brigade.

W Lendale Bennett
1st Adj Drake

DRAKE BATTALION
11 AUG 1916
1ˢᵗ R.N. BRIGADE

Army Form C. 2118.

WAR DIARY
or
INTELLIGENCE SUMMARY.
(Erase heading not required.)

Instructions regarding War Diaries and Intelligence Summaries are contained in F. S. Regs., Part II. and the Staff Manual respectively. Title pages will be prepared in manuscript.

Place	Date	Hour	Summary of Events and Information	Remarks and references to Appendices
COUPIGNY.	July 1st	8pm	A & B. Coy's left COUPIGNY at 8pm, and relieved & left 2 Coy's of 15th London Regt for instructional purposes. They arrived at 12 midnight in SOUCHEZ L Sector. WWS	
" "	July 4th		A & B. Coy's relieved by C & D Coy's midnight and returned to huts in COUPIGNY. WWS	
" "	July 5th		C & D Coy's left trenches and returned to COUPIGNY. WWS	

Army Form C. 2118.

WAR DIARY
or
INTELLIGENCE SUMMARY.
(Erase heading not required.)

Instructions regarding War Diaries and Intelligence Summaries are contained in F.S. Regs, Part II. and the Staff Manual respectively. Title pages will be prepared in manuscript.

Place	Date	Hour	Summary of Events and Information	Remarks and references to Appendices
COUPIGNY	July 1st	8 pm	A and B. Coy's left COUPIGNY to be attached to 15th London Reg's for instructional purposes in the trenches in the SOUCHEZ I sector. They arrived in the trenches at 12 midnight. MM	
"	July 2nd	12.45am	Raid by 15th Londons at 12.45am. Party consisted of 70 men and 6 officers which were split up into two parties. Raid was a failure, and the officers put down the cause to a certain German listening post. Only the right party got anywhere near the trenches which however they did not penetrate. Casualties in the raiding parties were slight, but there were a good many in the trenches in the trenches caused by the German artillery retaliation which lasted for half-an-hour. A & B Coy's casualties – A. Coy. nil. B. Coy OR: 1 killed & 2 wounded. MM	
"	July 4th	00	A. and B. Coy's relieved by C & D Coy's at about midnight, and returned to Huts in COUPIGNY. C Coy. 2OR. wounded. D. Coy. nil. MM Rgtl Order Para 2. hub P DX entitled to command pay from 16/1/16 – 26/2/16. D.R.O 228	
	July 5th		C & D Coy's left trenches and returned to COUPIGNY. MM	
	July 7			

T2134. Wt. W708—776. 500000. 4/15. Sir J.C. & S.

WAR DIARY or INTELLIGENCE SUMMARY

Army Form C. 2118.

Place	Date	Hour	Summary of Events and Information	Remarks and references to Appendices
Souchez	July 6th		Nomenclature "Grenade Battn" known in future as "Grenade Bn". See Orders Para 4. MHA Command Pay (Lieut PDIX) D.R.O. 228 cancelled MHA	
" "	July 7th		C.R.D. Cay left Souchez I Sector and returned to Courrieres v. MH	
" "	July 8th		D.R.O. 248. Temporary commission and appointment of Lieut A.M. Maclean RNVR Grenade Bn terminated owing to medical unfitness to date 23rd July 1916. MH	
July 13.			D.R.O. 264 Acting Major A Stuttig, 2nd R.M.Battalion attached to Grenade Battn from this date. MH Battalion left Courrieres about 8 pm and took over from 16th London Regiment in Souchez II Section Relief complete 1.15 am 11.15. MH	

WAR DIARY
INTELLIGENCE SUMMARY
(Erase heading not required.)

Army Form C. 2118.

Place	Date	Hour	Summary of Events and Information	Remarks and references to Appendices
Auchin	13th		Lt. Comm H.B. POLLOCK wounded by shrapnel. 2 O.R. wounded. WD/WS	
	13th	2am	Battalion relieved by 20th London Regiment and marched back to Yerbel. WD/WS	
	14th		DRO 246. (Temp/Major) A.S. Tetley appointed to command DRAKE BATT. pending confirmation of rank 12/7/16	
YERDREL	16th	9pm	Battalion left YERDREL at 9pm and marched to billets in BORIGNY ROUFFLES. WD/WS	
BORIGNY ROUFFLES	18th		Field G.C. wanted composed of President Commander W.C. Ramsay Raiston RN Hawke Batt. members Lieut. J.E. Allen Hood Batt. Sub Lt. J.E. Crowe Drake Batt. assembled for the trial of C.Z.3717. AS N SMITH who was found guilty on three charges and reduced to A.B. Williamson WD/WS	

WAR DIARY
or
INTELLIGENCE SUMMARY.
(Erase heading not required.)

Army Form C. 2118.

Place	Date	Hour	Summary of Events and Information	Remarks and references to Appendices
HQ B. BOUFFLERS	14th	8 pm	Battalion marched to ABLAIN ST NAZAIRE and occupied the support trenches on the LORETTE RIDGE. Work was carried on towards the improvement of the trenches. The Batt. relieved was the 18th London Regt. Situation normal during the 6 days. IWS	
ABLAIN ST NAZAIRE.			Resignation D.R.O. 318. Brigade Humorous as 184th Brigade. IWS Command Pay D.R.O. 314. Substitution for D.R.O. 228. of 5/7/16. Lt P. Quinn m entitled to command pay whilst in command of Batt. B.T.M during absence of command H.D. King D.S.O. on leave from 14/2/16 - 26/2/16 both dates inclusive. IWS	
	21st		Correction D.R.O. 246. 14/7/16 should read "Captain and Temporary Major A.S. letter to command Batt. B.T.M. voluntarily relinquishes 14/7/16 vice command H.D. King D.S.O. V.D RNVR to England for sea service." IWS Transfer D.R.O. 324. 21/7/16 command H.D. King D.S.O. VD RNVR to England for sea service Late 14/7/16. IWS Striking off Strength D.R.O. 326 T/2 Lieut A.P. Palmer RNVR Batt Batt.	

T2134. Wt. W708—776. 500000. 4/15. Sir J. C. & B.

Army Form C. 2118.

WAR DIARY
or
INTELLIGENCE SUMMARY.
(Erase heading not required.)

Instructions regarding War Diaries and Intelligence Summaries are contained in F.S. Regs., Part II. and the Staff Manual respectively. Title pages will be prepared in manuscript.

Place	Date	Hour	Summary of Events and Information	Remarks and references to Appendices
ABLAIN	July 25	—	Struck off the strength. Accidentally wounded 30/6/16 4th	
	26th		Relieved the HOOD BATTn in SOUCHEZ I Sector. Relief complete 1.15 am	
TRENCHES SOUCHEZ I Sector.			Situation quiet throughout. General improvements to the Trenches. 1 man accidentally wounded.	
	July 31st August 1st		Relieved by the HOOD Battn in Souchez I Sector. Relief complete 12 midnight. Battalion returned to ABLAIN ST NAZAIRE and occupied hutments on the LORETTE RIDGE.	

To Officer i/c.
   A.C's Office, Base.
From C.C. Drake Bn.

1/9/16.

Submitted; August War
Diary Volume 3 of the
Drake Bn.

for C.C. Drake Bn.
R.W.Bennell
(Sub Lt. & asst. Adjt.)

169
73 Army Form C. 2118.
Drake Bn.
Vol 2

WAR DIARY

INTELLIGENCE SUMMARY.
(Erase heading not required.)

Place	Date	Hour	Summary of Events and Information	Remarks and references to Appendices
ABLAIN ST. NAZAIRE	1.8.16		Battalion relieved by Hood Bn. during last night & early this morning & occupied reserve trenches on Lorette Ridge. Work carried out in improvement of these trenches during following six days.	
	2.8.16		—	
	3.8.16		Slight bombardment of DUGOUT LINE between 10 & 11 A.M. Shells dropped short. Effectively 1 m. wounded.	
	4.8.16		About 6 shrapnel shells burst near Ablain Church — one in the tower at 9-30 A.M.	
	5.8.16		—	

Army Form C. 2118.

Drake Bn.

WAR DIARY
INTELLIGENCE SUMMARY.
(Erase heading not required.)

Place	Date	Hour	Summary of Events and Information	Remarks and references to Appendices
ABLAIN ST NAZAIRE	6.8.16		Several shells fired into Ablain village at 11A.M. – mostly between Church & Bn. H.Q. Bn. relieved Hood Bn. in Souchez I sector. – Relief completed about 12.30.A.M. Ru.B	
SOUCHEZ I SECTOR	7.8.16		Bn. relieved by Hawke Bn. in Ansloy & tochn.	
SOUCHEZ I SECTOR.	7.8.16		One Coy of H.A.C. attached to Bn. for instructional purposes. Ru.B	
	8.8.16			
	9.8.16		H.A.C. relieved by another Coy of same regiment. Ru.B	

Army Form C. 2118.

Drake Bn.

WAR DIARY
or
INTELLIGENCE SUMMARY.
(Erase heading not required.)

Instructions regarding War Diaries and Intelligence Summaries are contained in F. S. Regs., Part II. and the Staff Manual respectively. Title pages will be prepared in manuscript.

Place	Date	Hour	Summary of Events and Information	Remarks and references to Appendices
Souchez I Sector	10.8.16		Enemy active with L.T.M's - Rifle Grenades in particular. Two killed. OR B	
	11.8.16		Enemy very active in Sector with L.T.M's & Rifle Grenades in particular. One killed, three wounded. OR B	
	12.8.16		Bn. relieved by Hood Bn. - Relief complete about 12 midnight. One killed, no wounded. OR B	
ABLAIN ST. NAZAIRE	13.8.16		Bn. attached by Hood Bn. - Relief complete about 12 midnight. OR B	
ABLAIN ST. NAZAIRE	14.8.16		Bn. relieved by Nelson Bn. - Relief complete about 1-30 A.M. Bn. marched to Aix Noulette Wood. OR B	

T2134. Wt. W708—776. 500000. 4/15. Sir J.C. & S.

Army Form C. 2118.

WAR DIARY
of
Drake Bn.
INTELLIGENCE SUMMARY.
(Erase heading not required.)

Instructions regarding War Diaries and Intelligence Summaries are contained in F. S. Regs., Part II. and the Staff Manual respectively. Title pages will be prepared in manuscript.

Place	Date	Hour	Summary of Events and Information	Remarks and references to Appendices
AIX NOULETTE				
Noo 0	15.8.16		Bn in huts. Numerous working parties supplied R.E.	
	16.8.16		ditto	
	17.8.16		ditto	
	18.8.16		ditto	
	19.8.16		xx "C" Coy Bn relieved Hood Bn - Souchez I Sector. Relief complete about 1.30 a.m. Ho. A. B. Coys attacked. "C" Coy went to Bouvigny Wood.	

Army Form C. 2118.

WAR DIARY
or
INTELLIGENCE SUMMARY.

Drake Bn.

(Erase heading not required.)

Place	Date	Hour	Summary of Events and Information	Remarks and references to Appendices
SOUCHEZ I SECTOR	20/8/16		A bombardment & gas release started in the ANGRES SECTOR at 10.30 p.m. which lasted till about 11.45 p.m. Some of the enemy retaliation with rifle & trench mortars were directed at our front & killer lines. Damage slight. Three wounded.	WB
	21.8.16		One wounded.	WB
	22.8.16		Aerial torpedos active about 9 a.m. on front line to right of Northumberland Avenue — damage slight. "B" Coy removed to billets at Aix Noulette for working parties. One killed. Two wounded.	WB
	23.8.16		Two wounded	WB
	24.8.16			

Army Form C. 2118.

WAR DIARY
INTELLIGENCE SUMMARY.

(Erase heading not required.)

Drake Bn.

Instructions regarding War Diaries and Intelligence
Summaries are contained in F. S. Regs., Part II.
and the Staff Manual respectively. Title pages
will be prepared in manuscript.

Place	Date	Hour	Summary of Events and Information	Remarks and references to Appendices
SOUCHEZ I SECTOR	25.8.16		Bn relieved by Hood Bn. – Relief complete about 11 p.m. Bn returned to Aix Noulette Wood.	
			"B" Coy " " " " " " R.W.F.	
AIX NOULETTE WOOD.	26.8.16		Bn in huts. Various working parties supplied during most six days. R.W.F.	
	27.8.16		One killed, one wounded, party whilst on working parties.	
	28.8.16			
	29.8.16			
	30.8.16			
	31.8.16		Bn. on A Coy relieved Hood Bn in Souchy I sector. A Coy moved to dilled in Aix Noulette for working parties.	

R.W. Simpson Lt
(Asst Adjutant)
for Lt Col A. Asquith
Comdg Drake Bn

To / Officer i/c. A. ep Office.
　　　　Base.
From, C.O.,
　　　　Drake Bn.　　　　　　1.10.16

　　Submitted herewith, Drake Bn.
War Diary. Vol. 4. for month of
September.

　　　　　　　　　A.S.
　　　　　　　　　Major R.M.L.I.
　　　　　　　　　O/c Drake Bn.

Army Form C. 2118.

Vol 3

Drake Bn.

WAR DIARY
INTELLIGENCE SUMMARY
(Erase heading not required.)

Place	Date	Hour	Summary of Events and Information	Remarks and references to Appendices
	Sept.			
Souchez 1 SECTOR	1		Took over sector from Howe Bn. midnight 31/8/16. This sector occupied by Bn. until night 6/7th when we were relieved by Howe Bn. just before midnight. Nothing of note to report during the six days up. Division quiet. Two wounded.	Drake B
	7			
LORETTE SECTOR	7		Occupied in early morning. This sector occupied by Bn. until night 12/13th.	Drake B
Souchez 1 SECTOR	13		Took over sector from Howe Bn. - relief complete 11.27 p.m. 12/9/16. 1 wounded.	Drake B
	14		Sector somewhat heavily bombarded between 9.50 to 10.35 p.m. by the enemy with shrapnel + some H.E. This no doubt was part of their retaliation in the raid on part of VIMY. We had eleven casualties.	Drake B

Army Form C. 2118.

WAR DIARY

INTELLIGENCE SUMMARY

(Erase heading not required.)

Instructions regarding War Diaries and Intelligence Summaries are contained in F.S. Regs., Part II. and the Staff Manual respectively. Title pages will be prepared in manuscript.

Drake Bn.

Place	Date	Hour	Summary of Events and Information	Remarks and references to Appendices
	15		Enemy retaliated to our French Trench Mortars at midday with L.T.M's. 1 killed & Trenches damaged somewhat.	App.B
Souchez Sector	16		During bombardment on VIMY between 1.30 and 2 A.M. the enemy again sent over a number of shells in this sector to which we replied with artillery. Damage Nil in our trenches.	App.B App.C
	17		Enemy retaliation to our Mortars during afternoon caused about seven casualties, but they may not a very fair one.	App.B
	18		Quiet day. Bn. was relieved about 11p.m. by 8th. Bn. Somerset Light Infantry & marched to Bouvigny Wood Huts where the Dugout Platoon, Lewis Gun Party, Tunnelling Party rejoined the Bn.	App.B
BOUVIGNY WOOD HUTS	19		At Bouvigny Wood Huts — wet day.	App.B
	20		Bn. marched from Bouvigny Wood Huts to billets at Hersilliers. Started at 8-15 A.M. and arrived at Hersilliers at 2-30 p.m. Bn. transport section joined up en route & the Brigadier reviewed the companies en route.	App.B

Army Form C. 2118.

WAR DIARY
or
INTELLIGENCE SUMMARY.
(Erase heading not required.)

Drake Bn.

Instructions regarding War Diaries and Intelligence Summaries are contained in F. S. Regs., Part II. and the Staff Manual respectively. Title pages will be prepared in manuscript.

Place	Date	Hour	Summary of Events and Information	Remarks and references to Appendices
FREVILLERS.	21/30		These ten days were devoted to Company, Battalion, Brigade and Divisional field training, concluding with a Brigade Route March (30th) of about nine miles. During period two parties of sixty men went to an exhibition of "Flammenwerfer". Lt. Dix resumed command of "A" company on 30th.	Appx. Appx.

Wedd,
Major Wedd
O/Drake Bn.

Confidential.

Drake Bn. No. 2
Nov. 1st. 1916.

War Diary (Volume V)

of

Drake Battalion

from

1st. Oct. 1916

to

31st. Oct. 1916.

To Headquarters
189th. Infantry Bde.

A.Tetley
Lt Col R.M.L.I.e
O.C. Drake Bn.

WAR DIARY

INTELLIGENCE SUMMARY.

Army Form C. 2118.

Drake Bn.

Place	Date	Hour	Summary of Events and Information	Remarks and references to Appendices
FREVILLERS	1/3		The Bn. continued training here.	
—	4		Bn. left here at 3 A.M. marched to Ypry at Herlin station where it entrained for FORCEVILLE arriving there at 8 p.m. Billeted in FORCEVILLE at 11-30 p.m.	
FORCEVILLE	5/4		The Bn. trained here	
—	8		The Bn. left here at 2 A.M. and marched to ENGLEBELMER where it was billetted by 4.30 A.M. The transport section and the Q.M.S. remained at FORCEVILLE.	
ENGLEBELMER	9/15		A certain amount of training was done but large working parties were supplied for the line nightly chiefly digging gun emplacements and carrying ammunition.	
—	16		The Bn. relieved 14th Bn Hants Regt in Y RAVINE SECTOR: relief complete 10-40 P.M.	

Army Form C. 2118.

WAR DIARY
INTELLIGENCE SUMMARY.
(Erase heading not required.)

Drake Bn.

Place	Date	Hour	Summary of Events and Information	Remarks and references to Appendices
Y RAVINE SECTOR	19		The Bn. was relieved by 1/4th Hertfs taking over line by 1.30 p.m. The Bn. returned to ENGLEBELMER occupying different billets those left the previous day. 1 Wounded.	
ENGLEBELMER	18/20		Working parties supplied for the line. 3 Wounded (19th) 1 Killed, 1 Missing + 2 Wounded (20th) } Digging assembly trench in sunken lane in	
MESNIL	21		Bn. marched here in morning and billeted in cellars in the village. Working parties supplied for line.	
—	22		2 Killed, 1 Officer + 3 men wounded. Digging assembly trench afronts. Working parties on line	
—	23		Bn. returned to ENGLEBELMER occupying different billets to those when last there.	
ENGLEBELMER	24/6		Bn. did certain amount of training	

Army Form C. 2118.

Drake Bn.

WAR DIARY
OF
INTELLIGENCE SUMMARY.
(Erase heading not required.)

Instructions regarding War Diaries and Intelligence Summaries are contained in F. S. Regs., Part II. and the Staff Manual respectively. Title pages will be prepared in manuscript.

Place	Date	Hour	Summary of Events and Information	Remarks and references to Appendices
HAMEL SECTOR	29/9		Bn relieved Hawke Bn in trenches. Relief complete 2 p.m.	Sat.
			3 killed and 2 wounded (27th)	
	30.		Bn relieved by 5th Royal Fusilier Bn. Relief complete 1 p.m. Bn marched to Cillo at HEADAUVILLE.	Sat.
HEADAUVILLE	31.		Bn (except D Coy who remained behind) left here at 10.15 a.m. marched to billets at PUCHEVILLERS.	Sat.

A. Nelson
Lt Col R.M.L.I.
O.C. Drake Bn.

CONFIDENTIAL.

Drake Bn.
Dec. 2nd 1916.

War Diary
of
Drake Bn.,
from
1 - 11 - '16
to
30 - 11 - '16.

Volume VI.

Wendell Bennett
LIEUT. R.N.V.R.
C.O. Drake Bn.

1893 Drake Bn. Vol 5

Army Form C. 2118.

WAR DIARY
of
INTELLIGENCE SUMMARY.
(Erase heading not required.)

Place	Date	Hour	Summary of Events and Information	Remarks and references to Appendices
PUICHVILLERS	Oct.?	1/5	A certain amount of training was done this.	
			Brigadier-Gen. L. F. Phillips, D.S.O. reviewed the Officers of the 189th. Infty. B'de. and also inspected the Transport lines of this Bn.	
			Major Gen. Shute C.B. reviewed the Officers and Men of the 189th Infty. B'de.	
			On 5th. the Bn. marched to billets at HEDAUVILLE, leaving PUICHVILLERS at 9 A.M. and arriving at destination about 1 P.M.	Ap.B
HEDAUVILLE	6		The Bn. marched to tents near ENGLEBELMER leaving HEDAUVILLE at 3 P.M. and arriving at destination at 4.50 P.M.	Ap.B
ENGLEBELMER	7/12		The Bn. remained here, supplying numerous working parties for the line. About 3.15 P.M. four men were wounded.	
			On the 12th. the Bn. left camp and took up their position in the gully in front of the HAMEL SECTOR at 9 P.M. in readiness for the attack against BEAUCOURT-SUR-ANCRE the following morning. Our "more elaborate" codename until ZERO. During the night our position was slightly shelled and "minnied".	Ap.B

Army Form C. 2118.

Drake Bn.

WAR DIARY
or
INTELLIGENCE SUMMARY.
(Erase heading not required.)

Place	Date	Hour	Summary of Events and Information	Remarks and references to Appendices
In front of HAMEL SECTOR.	Nov. 13	5.45 A.M.= ZERO.	Guns on left bank of river ANCRE commenced slightly before our barrage which caused the enemy to open minenwerfer fire at ZERO, when our men advanced. Barbed wire in front of enemy front line was thick in places making it necessary to pass through the gaps in small parties. Enemy front line was passed over and appeared to have been unoccupied by the enemy. Second line was found to be occupied by small parties on the left of our sector. While passing through this line Lieut. Col. A.S. Tetley was mortally wounded and several other officers were also killed and wounded. Owing to the mist and darkness combined with the smoke and dust, direction and control became extremely difficult. The third enemy trench was passed over without opposition and the advance continued with a mixture of the Drake Bn., Hood Bn., and a Bn. of the Honourable Artillery Company toward the GREEN LINE. About 6.15 A.M. daylight set in and the STATION became visible on our right. We changed direction half right and captured the STATION, meeting with M.G. opposition, and enemy M.G. and ammunition were captured and used against the enemy.	R.M.B.

Army Form C. 2118.

WAR DIARY
INTELLIGENCE SUMMARY
(Erase heading not required.)

Drake Bn.

Instructions regarding War Diaries and Intelligence Summaries are contained in F. S. Regs., Part II. and the Staff Manual respectively. Title pages will be prepared in manuscript.

Place	Date	Hour	Summary of Events and Information	Remarks and references to Appendices
	Nov. 13 (continued)		One hundred and two prisoners were captured in dugouts behind the right of the ridge Q.18.a.9.5. The barrage was followed closely by the first and second waves until the GREEN LINE was captured. In order to strengthen the Hawk Bn. for the advance against the YELLOW LINE the Drakes advanced with the Hawks. On arriving at about 100 yards from the YELLOW LINE no further advance was possible owing to our own barrage still dwelling on that line. We started to consolidate our position and during the work orders were received from the Brigade that the barrage would not lift from YELLOW LINE owing to troops on our left being held up. At this time we lost one officer and several men killed, owing to our own barrage falling about 100 yards short of YELLOW LINE. It appeared that the YELLOW LINE was not occupied and we were convinced that BEAUCOURT could have been captured and the final objective attained. During the afternoon of the 13th the enemy appeared to occupy the YELLOW LINE and his M.G.s and snipers became active which caused delay in consolidating and wiring of our position. Up till about	Ap. B

Army Form C. 2118.

WAR DIARY
INTELLIGENCE SUMMARY
(Erase heading not required.)

Place: Drake Bn.

Date	Hour	Summary of Events and Information	Remarks and references to Appendices
Nov. 13/14	(continued) 7 p.m.	The enemy artillery was feeble. After this the enemy's artillery opened with heavies and shrapnel and continued to subject our line to this fire until relieved. We were in support to the 4th D.N. during the capture of BEAUCOURT-SUR-ANCRE on the morning of 14th at 7.45. SUMMARY:- Our mens morale was excellent throughout the whole operation and they kept right up to the barrage without faltering. Although exhausted owing to the heavy condition of the ground, the men carried forward their trophies equipment, including the ten Battalion Lewis Guns which were invaluable in the defence of our position. Supply of bombs and ammunition was good. A captured enemy ration dump was found of great value. Enemy tools and braded wire were used to great effect. The rum supplied us with water, and captured rum was issued to the men. The relief arrived at 2.0 a.m. on the morning of the 15th. Throughout the operation the 99th Div. were pushing on our immediate right, and the 188th bgde. B'dn on our left with the 190th bgde. B'dn in Divisional Reserve.	

WAR DIARY
INTELLIGENCE SUMMARY

Army Form C. 2118.

Drake Bn.

Place	Date	Hour	Summary of Events and Information	Remarks and references to Appendices
			During these operations this Bn. lost the following Officers:—	
			KILLED.	
			Lt. Commander P.S. Campbell.	
			Sub. Lt. J. N. M. Newall.	
			" Lt. Langford.	
			" H.A. Water.	
			DIED OF WOUNDS.	
			Lt. Col. A.S. Tetley.	
			MISSING BELIEVED KILLED.	
			Sub Lt. B.W.R. Bradley.	
			WOUNDED	
			Lt. J.W. Turrell.	
			Sub Lt. W.S. Pennett.	
			" D.F.Y. Philpot.	
			" A.E. Dovell.	
			" Harley.	
			" G.W. Whittaker.	
			" R.Y. Rollinson.	
			SHELL SHOCK	
			Lt. S.B. Constable.	
			In addition to the above, the following casualties occurred in the ranks:—	
			15 KILLED. 151 WOUNDED. 28 MISSING. 1 DIED OF WOUNDS. 1 SHELL SHOCK.	
	Nov. 15.		After being relieved the Bn. where to the original enemy front line trenches about 4 A.M. in front of HAMEL SECTOR and then rested in the dugouts until 9-30 A.M.	Cont'd

Army Form C. 2118.

WAR DIARY

INTELLIGENCE SUMMARY.

(Erase heading not required.)

Drake Bn.

Place	Date	Hour	Summary of Events and Information	Remarks and references to Appendices
	Nov. 15		(continued) they marched back via HAMEL and MESNIL to ENGLEBELMER which was reached about 12 noon. At 2-30 p.m. the Bn. marched to HEDAUVILLE & about 9 p.m. were taken in motor lorries to billets at ARQUEVES: arrived just before midnight. 60 reinforcements joined us at HEDAUVILLE.	Aug.B
ARQUEVES.	16/17		Bn. remained here. On afternoon of 17th inst. Brigadier-Gen. L.F. Phillips. D.S.O. reviewed and addressed the remaining Officers and Men at 12 p.m. hefty Bde.	Aug.B App.B
	18		Bn. left for DOULLENS at 9 a.m. and arrived at DOULLENS at 2-30 p.m. in lorries	App.B
DOULLENS.	19.		Bn. left for CANDAS at 10-10 A.M. and arrived at CANDAS at 1 p.m. 39 reinforcements joined us at CANDAS at 9 p.m.	App.3
CANDAS.	20.		Maj. Gen Shute reviewed the 189th hty. Bde. at FIENVILLERS during morning. The Bn. together with the other Bns. was inspected by Gen. Sir Douglas Haig - Commander-in-Chief, at CANDAS in the afternoon 3-25 P.M.	Aug.B
	21		Bn. left CANDAS at about 10 A.M. and arrived at DOMQUEUR in billets ST.RIQUEUR at Anytime	Aug.B
DOMQUEUR	22.		Bn. left DOMQUEUR at about 9-45 P.M. and arrived at ST. RIQUEUR at 12 noon.	Aug.B
ST.RIQUER	23.		Bn. left ST. RIQUER at about 10 A.M. and arrived in billets at ST.OUENS HAUTVILLERS at 4-15 p.m.	App.B

Army Form C. 2118.

WAR DIARY
INTELLIGENCE SUMMARY.
(Erase heading not required.)

Drake Bn.

Instructions regarding War Diaries and Intelligence Summaries are contained in F. S. Regs., Part II. and the Staff Manual respectively. Title pages will be prepared in manuscript.

Place	Date	Hour	Summary of Events and Information	Remarks and references to Appendices
HAUTVILLERS.	Nov. 24		Bn. left HAUTVILLERS at 9A.M. and arrived in huts at ST.QUENTIN at 4.30 p.m.	RylB.
ST.QUENTIN	25/30		Bn. started strict allround training here. 151 reinforcements joined up.	RylB

Wendall Sewer R.N.V.R.
Lieut.
Commanding Officer Drake Bn.
(2-12-16)

WAR DIARY
or
INTELLIGENCE SUMMARY.

Army Form C. 2118

DRAKE B^N Vol 6

Place	Date	Hour	Summary of Events and Information	Remarks and references to Appendices
	Dec.			
S^T QUENTIN	1/26		Battalion carried out strict all round training.	
	27		Battalion left for LE CROTOY at 9.0 am	
LE CROTOY	29/31		Battalion continued training exercises	

Wendell Smith
Lieutenant RNVR
Commanding Drake Bⁿ

Army Form C. 2118.

Duke Batt.

WAR DIARY
or
INTELLIGENCE SUMMARY.
(Erase heading not required.)

Instructions regarding War Diaries and Intelligence Summaries are contained in F.S. Regs., Part II. and the Staff Manual respectively. Title pages will be prepared in manuscript.

Place	Date	Hour	Summary of Events and Information	Remarks and references to Appendices
LE CROTOY	Jan 11-14	—	Continuation of training though the Battn. HurK.	
"	12.1.15	—	Lt Colonel J.H.A. Annesley C.M.G. D.S.O. assumed command of the Battn. HurK.	
"	13th	—	Continuation of training through the Battn. HurK.	
"	14th	9.20am	Battalion moved off from LE CROTOY and marched to HAUTVILLERS.	
HAUTVILLERS	"	4.35 PM	Battn. arrived at HAUTVILLERS and billeted for the night. HurK	
"	15th	9am	Battn. moved off from HAUTVILLERS and marched to NOYELLE (via Chausse).	
NOYELLE	"	11.45 PM	Battn. arrived at NOYELLE and billeted for the night. HurK.	
"	16th	8.30am	Battn. moved off from NOYELLE and marched to CANDAS.	
CANDAS	"	5 PM	Battn. arrived at CANDAS and billeted for the night. HurK.	
"	17th	—	Battn. resting at CANDAS. Sub-Lt Hillkirk joined Battn. HurK.	
"	18th	9 am	Battn. moved off from CANDAS for RUBEMPRÉ.	
RUBEMPRÉ	"	2.30 PM	Battn. arrived at RUBEMPRÉ and billeted for the night. HurK.	
"	18th	12.30	Battn. moved off from RUBEMPRÉ by elbon bus for the trenches. B Coy left behind awaiting instructions to proceed to THIEPVAL.	
HAMEL	"	7.45 PM	Arrived at HAMEL and met guides from Duke of Wellingtons Battn.	
"	"	9.30 PM	Relief complete. A Coy in Reserve. C & D Coys in front line. Slight artillery duels. NoKow Battn on left. R.M. Battn on right. 1 O.R. Killed. HurK.	

Army Form C. 2118.

Drake Battn

WAR DIARY
or
INTELLIGENCE SUMMARY.

(Erase heading not required.)

Instructions regarding War Diaries and Intelligence Summaries are contained in F. S. Regs., Part II. and the Staff Manual respectively. Title pages will be prepared in manuscript.

Place	Date	Hour	Summary of Events and Information	Remarks and references to Appendices
IN FRONT OF BEAUCOURT SECTOR.	19-1-17		Situation unchanged. 1 O.R. wounded. Intermittent Artillery duels.	
	20-1-17		Situation unchanged. Artillery duels. Front line Coys employed in improving Sulva trench. H.u.K.	
"	21-1-17		Situation unchanged. Heavy shelling by enemy in Sulva trench during the morning 10 till 11.30. Our Artillery replied in retaliation. Slight aeroplane activity. 2 O.R. killed. 1 P.O. wounded. 1 O.R. wounded. H.u.K.	
"	22-1-17	9:30 P.M	Situation unchanged. Artillery duels. 5:15 P.M. Relieved by Hood Battn. Relief complete. Battn moved to Reserve. 2 killed. 9 wounded. H.u.K.	
(Reserve)	23-1-17		Battn in Reserve. Aeroplane activity. Slight Artillery duels. Enemy Bm. on left. Two Coys Drake and one Coy Hood's (attached) supplied as various working parties H.u.K. Battn in reserve. 3 Coys less one Platoon engaged as working party improving trenches. Slight Artillery duels. H.u.K.	
"	24-1-17			
"	25-1-17		Battn in Reserve. Working parties supplied at night for improvement of front line trenches. Considerable aeroplane activity. Slight Artillery duels. 1 O.R. accidentally wounded. H.u.K.	
"	26-1-17		Battn in Reserve. Slight Artillery combats. H.u.K. Enemy battn in diff. R.A. Battn on right.	

Army Form C. 2118.

WAR DIARY
or
INTELLIGENCE SUMMARY.
(Erase heading not required.)

Drake Battalion

Instructions regarding War Diaries and Intelligence Summaries are contained in F.S. Regs., Part II. and the Staff Manual respectively. Title pages will be prepared in manuscript.

Place	Date	Hour	Summary of Events and Information	Remarks and references to Appendices
Beaucourt Sector in Reserve.	27.1.17		Battn in reserve supplying various working parties for front line. occasional aeroplane activity and intermittent artillery combat.	
"	"	6.45PM	Relief by H.A.C. complete. Battalion moved off to billets at FOREEVILLE less B. Coy. who remained at THIEPVAL.	
FOREEVILLE	"	10.30PM	Battalion billeted at FOREEVILLE. HWK.	
"	28.1.17		Battn at FOREEVILLE. Training and supplying various working parties as required by Brigade. HWK	
"	29.1.17		As for 28th. HWK	
"	30.1.17		Battn at FOREEVILLE. various working parties supplied Company Training	
"	"	2.30PM	B Company arrived FOREEVILLE from THIEPVAL and billeted. HWK	
"	31.1.17		Company training and various working parties supplied.	
"	"	10AM	Colonel B. N. DESLEY, CMG. DSO evacuated sick to Hospital MAJOR I.G.FREELAND assumed Command of the Battalion. HWK.	

31.1.17

J. Freeland
Lieut Comdg Drake Battn

CONFIDENTIAL

Batt. Headquarters
Drake Batt.
63rd (R.N.) Div.

WAR DIARY
OF
"DRAKE"
BATTALION

FROM
1st Febr. 1917
TO
28th Febr. 1917

To: The A.G's Office
3rd Echelon

J.C. Freyland Lt Col
Officer Commanding
Drake Batt.

Army Form C. 2118.

DRAKE BATT.

WAR DIARY or INTELLIGENCE SUMMARY.

(Erase heading not required.)

Place	Date	Hour	Summary of Events and Information	Remarks and references to Appendices
Forceville	1-2-17	1.30	Batt. moved off to take over Beaucourt sector from 188th Bde. Met guides	
	"	5.30	at Hamel.	
	"	10 p.m.	Relief Complete 7135.	
Beaucourt HQ. Sub. Station	2nd	6 A.M.	Enemy aeroplane active 7135.	
"	"	11-12	Enemy artillery active on our front line system 7135.	
"	3rd	12 MD	Batt. when relieved by Hood Bttn. went into Beaucourt trench in Reserve	
"	3rd	2 a.m.	Batt. disposed as follows. A. Coy on the Rt. Front. B Coy on the left front. Three (3) platoons of C Coy in support and reserve. One (1) platoon at Country Clearing Station "D" Coy supplied carrying parties to Yorkshire Trench.	
	3rd	6 A.M.	Our artillery fairly active, firing bursts throughout the night on enemy line. North Barrage started at 8.30 p.m. but was replied to by our guns. 7135.	
		11 A.M.	Enemy artillery registering on Beaucourt, Lula and front line 7135.	
		3.15	Enemy aircraft active; seven machines were seen 7135.	

Army Form C. 2118.

WAR DIARY
or
INTELLIGENCE SUMMARY.
(Erase heading not required.)

DRAKE BATT

Place	Date	Hour	Summary of Events and Information	Remarks and references to Appendices
BEAUCOURT TRENCH	FEB. 3"	11 PM	Our artillery opened a heavy barrage on Puisieux & River trenches under which the Hood Batt on the right and Hawke Batt on the left advanced to the attack. The enemy offered attempted no counter barrage, but shelled our line of communication trs	
"	4th	6 AM	In accordance with 189th Inf. Bde Order 2860, Puisieux and River trenches were captured and consolidated. Several local counter attacks were beaten off. Estimated 2° of prisoners 120, chiefly of the 31st R.I.R., 84th Inv and 230th R.I.R. Barrage was reported to be satisfactory.	
		7/30 AM	Contact aeroplanes were over our lines working in connection with our artillery. The Klaxon horn was heard at intervals from the machines, it is reported that our guns had several direct hits on gun emplacements. tel	
		9 AM	Enemy artillery quiet during the day tel Reported that the Hawke Batt had captured the strong pont at R.2.a.6.65. which had given some trouble	

Army Form C. 2118.

DRAKE BATT.

WAR DIARY
or
INTELLIGENCE SUMMARY.
(Erase heading not required.)

Place	Date	Hour	Summary of Events and Information	Remarks and references to Appendices
BEAUCOURT TRENCH.	FEB. 4TH	9 A.M.	during the attack on Beaucourt and River trenches NBS	
	"	10 A.M.	Enemy endeavoured to break our new line, attacking from the South along Miraumont-Beaucourt Road, Strength estimated at one company. They were repulsed with loss. Enemy shelled our position heavily NBS.	
		10.15 A.M.	S.O.S. signal from our lines, our artillery responded and opened an intense barrage, upon all the approaches to our newly gained ground. Barrage slackened at 11.30 A.M. NBS. Enemy artillery exceeding by active NBS Reported Lieut.	
		12 Noon	Lieut. Ede & Lt. Woodford wounded NBS.	
		9.30 P.M.	Enemy opened tremendous barrage on the whole sector particularly roads Hamel-Beaucourt, Beaucourt-Miraumont, under cover of which he again counter attacked Beaucourt and River trenches. Enemy were again beaten off with loss. Our own casualties among officers and men reported to be heavy.	

Army Form C. 2118.

DRAKE BATT

WAR DIARY
or
INTELLIGENCE SUMMARY.
(Erase heading not required.)

Instructions regarding War Diaries and Intelligence Summaries are contained in F.S. Regs., Part II. and the Staff Manual respectively. Title pages will be prepared in manuscript.

Place	Date	Hour	Summary of Events and Information	Remarks and references to Appendices
BEAUCOURT TRENCH.	4/5/18	MDNT.	For further details of operations see APPENDIX A. WD.	For further particulars
	5th	6AM	Front remained its normal quietness. WD.	3/5th 26rs.
	5th	6PM	Battalion moved into Reserve in Old German front line system of trenches at Q.18.C.59. (Map Ref. 57d S.E. 1/20,000)	
Old German Front line	6th June	6AM	Battalion supplied working and cleaning up parties for front line. Enemy artillery quiet. WD.	see APPENDIX "A"
	"	6PM	Battalion roll call. 2pm. WD. O'C inspection and congratulations to troops. WD.	
	7th	6AM	Burial parties. WD.	
	7th	6PM	Battalion regarding reorganising.	
	8th	11AM		
	8th	6PM		
	9th	6AM	Battalion regarding Route march. WD. General cleaning u/s parties supplied. WD.	
	9th	6PM		
	10th	5.30PM	Battalion relieved by Hood Battn. from Q.18.C.5.9. instructed to move to Donnet Post, and on arrival to report to Brigadier Transportation.	
		8.30PM	Arrived at Donnet Post 6x7a. Took over "Bow Huts" from	

Army Form C. 2118.

DRAKE BATT

WAR DIARY
or
INTELLIGENCE SUMMARY.
(Erase heading not required.)

Place	Date	Hour	Summary of Events and Information	Remarks and references to Appendices
DONNET'S POST	FEB. 10TH	8.30 AM	8th East Surrey Regiment. WBS.	
	11TH	7 AM	Reveille 7AM. Battalion given day to clean rifles, equipment, clothes, etc. WBS.	
	11TH	4 PM		
DO	12TH	6 AM	Working party 6 Officers and 290 O.R. for transportation work. WBS.	
		12 MDNT	Received orders Battalion to proceed to Paisley Dump (Q.30.C.8.3.) and take over dug outs in Thiepval wood, as DONNET'S POST was required for troops of the 7ND DIVISION. Relief to be carried out by 1pm. 13TH INST. WBS.	
DO	13TH	11AM	Battalion moved as ordered. WBS. Relief complete. Dug outs in Thiepval wood found to be inadequate for accomodating Battalion; they were found to be in a very bad condition. WBS. D Coy went sent to Q.18.C.59 for the night. WBS.	
	14TH	4/M	D. Coy billeted in village of Thiepval. Working parties supplied for transportation work. WBS.	
THIEPVAL WOOD.				
DO		2 MDNT	Enemy aircraft passed over Thiepval & Thiepval wood five bombs were dropped but no casualties were reported, no	

Army Form C. 2118.

DRAKE BATT.

WAR DIARY
or
INTELLIGENCE SUMMARY.
(Erase heading not required.)

Instructions regarding War Diaries and Intelligence Summaries are contained in F. S. Regs., Part II. and the Staff Manual respectively. Title pages will be prepared in manuscript.

Place	Date	Hour	Summary of Events and Information	Remarks and references to Appendices
THIEPVAL WOOD.	FEB. 14th	12 noon	Further evidence of intelligence procurable. W.D.S.	
"	15th	6 AM	Working party of 5 officers and 160 O.R. supplied for transportation work. Specialist training continued. Lewis gunners, bombers, and Observers. W.D.S.	
		6 PM	Enemy aeroplanes again active, no damage or casualties. Nothing. W.D.S.	
"	16th	6 AM	Working party of 2/14 O.R. & 5 officers supplied for transportation work. W.D.S. Tactical scheme for officers by O.C. Battn. B.189. I.R. to relieve HOOD BATT. in	
		2 noon	Received orders for Battn. B.189. I.R. to relieve HOOD BATT. in Old German Front Line Q.18.C.5,27. W.D.S.	
Old German Front Line.	17th	2 AM	Relief completed. W.D.S.	
		6/m	Battalion in Reserve 713/.	
	18th	6 AM	Working parties cancelled. W.D.S.	
	19th	6 AM	Working parties supplied totalling 5 officers and 220 O.R. W.D.S.	
Old German 3rd Line.	20th	6 AM	Batt. moved to 3rd Line Old German system. W.D.S.	
		6/m	Carrying parties supplied to 188 Inf. Bde.	

Army Form C. 2118.

WAR DIARY
or
INTELLIGENCE SUMMARY.
(Erase heading not required.)

DRAKE BATT.

Place	Date	Hour	Summary of Events and Information	Remarks and references to Appendices
Old German 3rd Line	Feb. 20th	6 p.m.	Battalion received orders to move back into Old German line system N.3.d.	
Old German 2nd Line	21st	1 p.m.	Battalion completed movement as ordered N.3.d. Working parties supplied to "190th Inf. Bde."	
"	22nd	6 a.m.	Working parties supplied to "190th Inf. Bde." carrying rations to front line N.3.d.	
"	"	12 noon	General Lawrie in command 63rd (R.N.) Div. vacated Batt. lines N.3.d.	
"	23rd	6 a.m.	Carrying parties supplied to 190th Inf. Bde. also party supplied to clean out dug outs and trenches which Battalion was occupying N.3.d.	
Miraumont	24th	Mdnt.	Battalion received orders to move to Beaucourt Caves. Acting in reserve to 190th Inf. Bde. who were advancing to wards Miraumont N.3.8.	
"	24th	2 a.m.	Battalion completed movement as ordered N.3.8.	
Beaucourt Caves	25th	6 a.m.	Battalion received orders to move to Sunken Road [R.9.9.?] acting in reserve to 190th Inf. Bde.	

DRAKE BATT

WAR DIARY
INTELLIGENCE SUMMARY
(Erase heading not required.)

Army Form C. 2118.

Place	Date	Hour	Summary of Events and Information	Remarks and references to Appendices
SUNKEN ROAD.	25th	6pm	Enemy artillery normal. 928. Four casualties: four killed 928.	BEAUCOURT TRENCH Sheet 57d.
"	26th	6am	Battalion received orders to ~~BEAUCOURT~~ move to ~~BEAUCOURT TRENCH~~ 92d.	
"	"	6pm	Battalion moved to BRUCE POST. 92d.	
BRUCE POST	27th	6am	Battalion received orders to move Quartermasters Stores and transport to BRUCE POST, 92d.	
"	"	6pm	Orders received for Battalion to move ~~to~~ into huts near O.11.4.5.95.	
"	"	9pm	Above orders cancelled and to take effect next day 28th inst	
"	28th	6am	Battalion moved to Camp near OVILLERS as ordered. 92b. Arrangement being made to have huts on route. On arrival at position hastily erected tents, and settled down. Working party of 5 Offs. and 250 OR. supplied for transportation work. 92b.	

1.3.17.

J Freyburg Lt Col
Y Cmdg Drake Battn

SECRET.   Drake Battalion Order No 5.   3.2.17.   APPENDIX. A.

Ref Trench Map 10,000
1.(a) The enemy is reported to be holding PUISIEUX and RIVER Trenches, both of which have been considerably damaged by shell fire, with 6 weak Coys of the 3rd Infy Regt.
(b) As far as is known the wire is practically non-existent.
(c) The morale of the enemy on our front is poor.
2.(a) The 189th Infy Bde is to capture PUISIEUX and RIVER Trenches from the River ANCRE to ARTILLERY ALLEY tonight, and dig a new line of trench to the East of RIVER Trench and North of ARTILLERY ALLEY.
(b) Time of ZERO will be notified later.
3.(a) The attack will be carried out by the HOOD BATTN (No 1 Battn) on the right, and the HAWKE BATTN (No 2 Battn) on the left.
(b) The NELSON BATTALION (No 3 Battn) will be in support with one company in the outpost line, Posts 11 to 16; one Coy in trench across PUISIEUX VALLEY at R.1.D.Central (known as YORKSHIRE Trench); one Coy in steel slits which have been dug from R.1.D.7.5. to R.7.B.5.5. and one Coy in West end of SUVLA TRENCH.
(c) The DRAKE BATTN. (No 4 Battn) will be in Reserve with one Coy in SUVLA TRENCH astride the BEAUCOURT-PUISIEUX Road, and remainder of Battn less carrying parties in Ravine in Q.12.D.
(d) The 7th Battn Royal Fusiliers (attached to the 189th Inf Bde for the operation) will be in reserve in the old German front line, in Q.18. A. and C.
4.(a) "A" Company on relief by the HOOD BATTN. will move to SUVLA Trench astride the BEAUCOURT-PUISIEUX Road, and come under the orders of the O.C. NELSON BATTN. to whom an officer will be sent

to report at Batt H.Q at R.7.A.2.2. in BEAUCOURT Trench as soon as the Coy is in position.

"B" Company less carrying parties, on relief by the HOOD and HAWKE Batts, will move to the RAVINE in Q.12.D.

"C" Coy. less carrying parties, will move at 8.00 P.M to the RAVINE in Q.12.D.

(b) "A" Coy will move forward at ZERO - 5 minutes and take the place of the Coy of the NELSON Batth in YORKSHIRE Trench. The latter is to move forward and consolidate ARTILLERY ALLEY.

At dawn "A" Coy, when relieved by a Coy of the NELSON Batth will move back and occupy dugouts in BEAUCOURT and BEAUCOURT Trench and will remain in close support ready to move at a moment's notice. They will not use the Cave.

"A" Coy will not move back from YORKSHIRE Trench until relieved.

(c) "B" and "C" Coys will not move from the RAVINE, except under orders from the O.C. and will be ready to move at 15 minutes notice.

5. "A" and "B" Coys will report to Battn HQn as soon as they are in position in SUVLA Trench and the RAVINE respectively.

6. Aid Post will be at R.7.B.8.1½. and R.1.D.6.5.
Advanced Bearer Post at Q.18.B.5.8 and in Cave at R.7.C.8.8.
Collecting Station for walking wounded in HAMEL
No unwounded men, except stretcher bearers, who will wear the recognised brassards, will on any account accompany wounded back to Aid Posts.
Any breach of this order will be severely dealt with

7. Prisoners will be sent to the junction of SUVLA Trench and PUISIEUX Road (R.7.B.7.8) where they

3

will be taken over by a special party and conducted to the Brigade Cage in RAVINE at O.12.D.

Any captured Machine Guns will be sent back with prisoners and carried by them to Brigade Cage.

8. "A" and "B" Coys will ensure that every commander, however subordinate, has an understudy, and that this understudy is known to all the men under his command

9. No papers except the special maps which have been issued and the 1/10000 Trench map, which convey any information of military value, will be carried into action. All copies of these orders will be returned to Battn H.Qrs at ZERO hour.

10. Any man found in possession of any trophy will be tried by Court Martial

11. The S.O.S. signal will be one White Rocket followed by one Red followed by one White.

12. Battn H Qrs will remain in its present position, where all reports will be sent.

Issued at 7.00 p.m.

Signed J.C. Freeland Major.
Temp. Commander Drake Battalion

No 1 Copy	189th Inf Bde
" 2 "	A Company
" 3 "	B "
" 4 "	C "
" 5 "	War Diary

Report on the action of the Drake Battn. in the operations of 3rd–5th Feb 1917 north of the River ANCRE.

In accordance with 189th Inf. Bde Order No. 60 and amendments, the DRAKE Battalion at ZERO hour (11 p.m.) on 3rd Feb. was disposed as follows:-
"A" Coy in YORKSHIRE TRENCH, under orders of O.C. NELSON Bn.
"B" Coy (less 2 Platoons employed on Carrying Parties) in the RAVINE, Q.12.D.
"C" Coy (less 2½ Platoons employed in carrying, 1 Section employed in Soup Kitchens, and 1 Platoon detached with the 149th C.C.S.)
"D" Coy employed on carrying and working parties.
Drake Battalion Order No. 5 ordering the above was issued at 4 p.m. on the 3rd Feb (vide Appendix "A").

The Battalion remained as above until about 10 a.m. on the morning of the 4th Feb. when orders were received from the G.O.C. 189th Inf. Bde. to move the Company ("A" Coy) from YORKSHIRE TRENCH to the Southern end of the PUISIEUX VALLEY near the Right Advanced Bde Dump, and the Company in the RAVINE, Q.12.D to BEAUCOURT TRENCH — preparatory to making a counter attack on the Hood's right, where the enemy were reported to have attacked, should the situation demand it.

The O.C. HOOD Battn. was communicated with regarding the situation on his front and right and replied that there appeared to be no necessity for a counter attack, as the early reports were much exaggerated and he thought the Battn. could deal with the situation without assistance.

"A" and "B" Coys. remained in the above positions all day, and the former suffered some casualties from the heavy barrage, which the enemy put on the PUISIEUX VALLEY during the early part of the afternoon.

At about 5 p.m. orders were received by wire that "A" Coy was to move up to PUISIEUX TRENCH in rear of the HOOD Battn., detaching 1 Platoon for employment under the orders of the O.C. HOOD Battn. to clear the enemy from a post which they seized in the HOOD Battn. front.

The two Coys employed on carrying parties ("C" and "D" Coys) were to be collected and moved up to PUISIEUX TRENCH in rear of the HAWKE Battn.

"B" Coy from BEAUCOURT TRENCH, reinforced if necessary by Platoons from "A" Coy was to move at once to fill a gap in the front line between the HOOD and HAWKE Battns. from R.2.D.8.5 to R.2.D.5.9. "B" Coy was to work along RIVER TRENCH from the HOOD's left cutting the communications of a German strong point which was holding out at R.2.D.4.5.

These orders were afterwards confirmed by 189th Inf. Bde Order No. 62.

Orders were at once issued to Companies to carry out the above operations and movements.

Action of "A" Coy.
"A" Coy moved to the outpost lines and occupied Posts 1 to 5. This was done under the orders of the O.C. HOOD Battn. to whom the O.C. "A" Coy was ordered to report for instructions regarding the 1 Platoon to be attached to the HOOD Battn. and also to find out where in PUISIEUX TRENCH the remainder of the Coy was to move. As soon as this was discovered, arrangements were made with the O.C. HOOD Battn. to move "A" Coy to PUISIEUX TRENCH

south of the BEAUCOURT - MIRAUMONT Road, and the Coy was ordered to move at once (about 4 pm).

The Coy was moved by its C.O. to the trench in rear of PUISIEUX TRENCH (R.8.B 36 to R.8.B 34) which it entered at about 8 pm. The Coy Commander leaving the Coy in the trench went along the trench towards point R.8.B.43, with the Commander of the Coy of the HOOD Battn. which was holding the right flank (Lt OLIVER) and the Platoon under Sub Lt HILLKIRK, which was to attack the post held by the enemy.

A few minutes after the arrival of the Coy in the trench (R.8.B.36 to 34) the enemy opened a barrage in rear of the trench, which lasted for about 4 minutes. Almost immediately after the barrage ceased, the Coy was attacked in rear and on the right flank by a strong party of the enemy with bombs and was completely surprised. Being crowded together in the trench with men of the Company of the Hood Battn., the casualties from the bombing were heavy. As many unwounded men as could be found were collected by the two remaining Officers of "A" Coy and a counter-attack to drive off the bombers was organized. By this time most of the enemy had retired and of those who remained to cover the retirement all were killed.

The Coy Commander, Lieut. RICHARDS and Sub Lieut HILLKIRK were both wounded and the whole of the Platoon which had gone up the trench towards point R.8.B.43. were killed, wounded or missing.

Immediate steps were taken to guard against a repetition of this bombing attack, and posts were established overlooking the river bed, in the trench from R.8.B.34 to R.8.B.43.

On receipt of information regarding the bombing attack, a Company of the 14th Worcesters (Pioneers) who were working in ANCRE TRENCH, were collected and sent forward with bombs for "A" Coy.

A report was sent to Bde HQ regarding the hostile attack, and the action taken in the matter, and at about 11.45 p.m. a Company of the 4th Bn. Royal Fusiliers, ("C" Coy) which was placed at my disposal, was sent forward from the old outpost line, to reinforce "A" Coy in PUISIEUX TRENCH and the trench in rear of it.

"A" Coy remained in this position until relieved in the early hours of the morning of the 6th Feb. by the 1st Bn. H.A.C. and moved back to the old German Front Line.

Action of "B" Coy.

"B" Coy moved up from BEAUCOURT TRENCH at 4 pm with orders to report at the Hood Bn. HQ, on the way to pick up guides, which had been arranged for. Lieut-Commander ASQUITH went up with the Coy and appears to have accompanied it during the operation which it had been detailed to carry out, until he was wounded. He appears to have taken command of the Company.

On arrival at the left flank of the HOOD Battn. in RIVER TRENCH it was reported to the Coy Commander by OC. Left Coy of the HOOD Battn. that the enemy were holding a post at about R.2.D.8.5. This was attacked and found to have been evacuated by the enemy. A post with a Lewis gun was placed at this point and the Company proceeded to work their way towards the HAWKE Battn. right, at about point R.2.D.5.9. A strong party of the enemy shortly afterwards approached the post at R.2.D.8.5. and were allowed to come quite close before being challenged. Fire was then opened on them and they were dispersed with heavy casualties.

A hostile machine gun had been reported by the HOOD Battn to have been in action at about point R.2.D.8².5¹. and a patrol was sent to reconnoitre in that direction. The machine gun was found abandoned and was brought in. This gun was found to be in working order and was used by "B" Company against the enemy with good effect during the time they were in the front line. The Company worked from shell hole to shell hole, being sniped and fired at by machine guns from both flanks, and consolidated a line of posts as they went. Some difficulty was experienced in locating the HAWKE Battn Right Flank, and on a report to that effect being received at Battn H.Q., the O.C. HAWKE Battn was asked to assist by firing VERY lights every 5 minutes from 4.15 am for ½ hour. A reply was received that this would be done if possible, but no VERY lights were fired.

The difficulty of "B" Company's task was increased by the fact that RIVER TRENCH which should have given them the 'line' was unrecognizable.

When the Company had pushed out about 150 yards, Sub Lieut LUNN, commanding the Coy, took out a patrol to try and locate the HAWKE Battn Right. None of the patrol were seen again & SUB Lieut POUND took command.

At 12.45 am a message was received to the above effect at Battn H.Q. stating that reinforcements were required to enable the operation to be carried through. Two Platoons of the Coy of the 4th Br Royal Fusiliers under an Officer were thereupon sent up from PUISIEUX TRENCH to assist "B" Coy.

At the same time a message was received from Bde H.Q. placing another Coy ("B" Coy) of the 4th Br Royal Fusiliers at my disposal. This Coy was ordered to move to Posts 1 to 5 of the old outpost line, and remain there until further orders. This Coy was kept in reserve until the night of the 5/6th Feb. when the 189th Inf. Bde was relieved.

At 10.30 am a message was received from "B" Coy DRAKE BATTN reporting that they had up to that time been unable to find the HAWKE Battn right flank. Orders were sent to the O.C. Coy to send out patrols in a westerly direction, as it was thought probable that the Coy had moved too much to their right, and make every endeavour to connect up as soon as possible.

At about 1 pm a message was received from the O.C. Coy that he had located the right of the HAWKE BATTN and was taking steps to join up with it.

At about 5 pm a message was received through the O.C. HOOD Battn that "B" Coy had retired from the line they were holding leaving the HOOD left flank in the front line in the air. Orders were at once sent to the O.C. B Coy to return to his former position as which was later reported to have been done. It appears that the right of "B" Coy retired through a misunderstanding.

"B" Coy were relieved by the 1st H.A.C. on the right as far as MIRAUMONT ALLEY and from there to the left by the 10th Bn. Dublin Fusiliers. at 5.0 a.m. on 6th Feb. and moved back to the old German Front Line System.

Action of "C" & "D" Coys

At 5 p.m. on the 4th Feb. orders were issued to the O's C. "C" & "D" Coys. to collect their Coys. and move them to POISIEUX TRENCH in rear of the HAWKE Battn. The O's C. Coys were ordered to report at the HAWKE Battn. H.Q. for instructions as to where to go in POSIEUX TRENCH and for guides to lead the Coys forward. Instead of this however, the O's C & D Coys received instructions from the O.C. HAWKE BATTN to help to fill a gap which existed in the front line between the HAWKE Battn left at R.2.B.0.6. and the NELSON Battn right. While the O's C. these Coys. were receiving their orders from the O.C. HAWKE Battn., the Companies were put into YORKSHIRE TRENCH.

While advancing up the POISIEUX VALLEY and also while in YORKSHIRE TRENCH, the two Companies came under a very heavy shell fire, from 5.9", 4.2", and 77 mm. guns, and suffered a considerable number of casualties, including both Coy Commanders (Lieut. Johnson and Sub Lieut SPARKS) and two other Officers. This left the two Coys. with only three Officers, two of whom were very junior and inexperienced. Sub Lieut FOX, therefore, took command of both Coys.

The two Coys. reduced considerably in strength, were guided forward and placed in position by the O.C. left Coy of the HAWKE Battn. They occupied and consolidated a line of shell hole posts.

The two Coys remained in this position until 12.30 a.m. on the night of the 5/6th Feb. when they were relieved by the 10th Bn. Dublin Fusiliers, and moved back to the old German Front Line System. No incident of interest occurred while they occupied the above portion of the line.

The Casualties in the Battn on the 3rd, 4th, 5th and 6th Feb. were mostly caused by shell fire and were :-

	Officers	Other Ranks
Killed	1	32
Died of Wounds	1	11
Wounded	8	102
Missing	1	67
Wounded & Missing	-	1
Shell Shock	-	2
Gas Poisoning	-	-
Total	11	201

Recommendations
for Reward

The Names of Officers and Other Ranks who distinguished themselves and whom I wish to recommend for immediate reward, have already been submitted.

(Signed) J.C. Freeland
Lt Col.
Commdg. Drake Battn.

Army Form C. 2118.

WAR DIARY
or
INTELLIGENCE SUMMARY.
(Erase heading not required.)

DRAKE BATT^N

Place	Date	Hour	Summary of Events and Information	Remarks and references to Appendices
SPRING GARDEN CAMP.	1-3-17 to		Battⁿ. encamped at SPRING GARDEN CAMP just SOUTH of OVILLERS. Daily working parties	
S. of OVILLERS	18-3-17		supplied on railway extensions varying from 300-600 men and 8 officers.	
"			Training of specialists carried out as far as possible. Hd^{rs}-K.	
"	3-3-17	4 P.M.	222 Reinforcements arrived from Entrenching Battalion. Hd^{rs}-K.	
"	11-3-17		Lt. Col. FREELAND Cmdg. Battⁿ attending special conference of four days at 5th Army School.	
"			DOMART-EN-PONTHIEU Hd^{rs}-K.	
"	16-3-17		Lt. Col. FREELAND returned from DOMART. Hd^{rs}-K.	
"	18-3-17		W. Col. FREELAND recalled to INDIA. Hd^{rs}-K.	
WARLOY	19-3-17	8.30 A.M	Battⁿ. moved off to billets at WARLOY.	
"	"	12.30 P.M.	Battⁿ arrived at WARLOY and billeted for the night. Hd^{rs}-K.	
VAL DE MAISON	20-3-17	9.30 A.M	Battⁿ. moved off to billets at VAL DE MAISON.	
"	"	2 P.M.	Arrived at VAL DE MAISON and billeted for the night. Hd^{rs}-K.	
VISÉE	21-3-17	9.45 A.M	Battⁿ moved off to billets at VISÉE. A+B Coys at VISÉE. C+D Coys. at RANSART.	
RANSART.	"	4.30 P.M	A+B. Coys. arrived at VISÉE.	
"	"	5.15 P.M	C+D Coys. arrived at RANSART. + billeted for the night. Hd^{rs}-K.	
NUNCQ	22-3-17	9 A.M	Battⁿ. moved off to billets at NUNCQ	

Army Form C. 2118.

WAR DIARY
or
INTELLIGENCE SUMMARY.
(Erase heading not required.)

DRAKE BATT[N]

Place	Date	Hour	Summary of Events and Information	Remarks and references to Appendices
NUNCQ	22.3.17	4.15PM	Batt. arrived at NUNCQ and billeted for two nights. 4thR.K.	
"	23.3.17	-	Batt. resting at NUNCQ. 10 reinforcements arrived and posted to Batt. 4thR.K.	
BOURS	24.3.17	9AM	Batt. moved off to billets at BOURS.	
"	"	2.30PM	Arrived at BOURS and billeted for the night. 4thR.K.	
RELY	25.3.17	10AM	Batt. moved off to billet at RELY.	
"	"	2.45PM	Arrived at RELY and billeted for the night 4thR.K.	
VENDIN-LEZ-BETHUNE	26.3.17	8.30AM	Batt. moved off to billets at VENDIN-LEZ-BETHUNE.	
"	"	6.30PM	Batt. billeted. A+B Coys at FOUQUEREUIL. 4thR.K.	
"	27.3.17	PM	Working party of 109 ORs and 2 officers supplied for VERDREL WOOD. 4thR.K.	
"	28.3.17	-	Batt. undergoing strict training.	
"	31.3.17	-	30" Working party supplied for VERDREL WOOD returned. 4thR.K.	

Henry S Cotton
Lt.
for O/C. Drake Batt[n]
63rd R.N. Division

Drake
Vol 10 of Drake Battn.

WAR DIARY or INTELLIGENCE SUMMARY

Army Form C. 2118.

Place	Date	Hour	Summary of Events and Information	Remarks and references to Appendices
VENDIN-LES-BÉTHUNE	April 1st 1917 – July 1st		The Battn thoroughly reorganised companies & carried out training	P.R.H.F.
"	April 3rd		Lieut Commander Buinett returned from England & resumed command	P.R.H.F.
HOUCHIN	8.4.17	10.15 am	The Battn moved to huts at Houchin & were under four hours notice to move up to the line.	P.R.H.F.
HOUCHIN	8.4.17 – 10.4.17		Battn carried out close order drill & open order drill	P.R.H.F.
FREVILLERS	11.4.17 – 13.4.17	10.00am 8.30 a.m	Battn moved at short notice to Frevillers arriving there until the 13th. I remained there until 13th. Battn marched to Ectrueile front orderly Escenres arriving Bn in	P.R.H.F.
Ecoivres	13.4.17		Battn moved up into close support to Nelson Battn in Ecoivres	
Pont-du-Jour	14.4.17		Battn relieving the Suffolk Regiment (Cambridgeshire) Brigade front was held by 1 Batln. Nelson in front but Drake close support March in reserve. Hood in general reserve. 4th Bn Worces on our right 190th Brigade on our left.	P.R.H.F.
"	15.4.17	10.55pm	Battn received orders to move up & dig in front from H S central – B 39 c 81. 7. 3	

Army Form C. 2118.

WAR DIARY
or
INTELLIGENCE SUMMARY.
(Erase heading not required.)

2nd Batt.

Place	Date	Hour	Summary of Events and Information	Remarks and references to Appendices
Pont du Jour	15.4.17	cont	Coy right of the road, D Coy left of road, C Coy dug a line from H4 & 2.5 - B28d 75, so as a support line. A Coy occupied German gun pits at H4A central as a reserve with Batt. H.Q. The operation was successfully accomplished by daylight with 10 R killed, 3 wounded. All Coys had dug out well down over 5'6" by day light. Brigade front now consisted of 2 Batts in front line, 2 Batts in support with 4 Jowans on our right. P.R.H.S.	
"	16.4.17		Orders were received for the night of the 16th/17th to occupy German line opposite FAVREUIL which was thought to be lightly held but this was cancelled owing to the wiring went. Instead assembly trenches were dug on right of road 250 yds from German wire, this was successfully accomplished without a casualty. P.R.H.S	
"	17.4.17		Relieved by 10nd Batt. took over two dug outs in Old German front line on the ARRAS-BAILLEUL road. Relief completed 3 a.m. P.R.H.S.	
"	18.4.17 20.4.17		Batts supplied working parties on the two roads P.R.H.S.	

Army Form C. 2118.

WAR DIARY
or
INTELLIGENCE SUMMARY.
(Erase heading not required.)

Irah Bath

Place	Date	Hour	Summary of Events and Information	Remarks and references to Appendices
GAVRELLE Sec.	21.4.17	5 p.m.	Batt. relieved Hood Batt. relief complete 11.20 p.m. Batt. H.Q. moved to gun pits on right of ARRAS-GAVRELLE road at H4 c 6.8. I.R.H.F.	
"	22.4.17		Preparations for attack on GAVRELLE. I.R.H.F.	
"	23.4.17	4.45 a.m.	Zero barrage opened & Irish & Irah advanced to the attack. Nelson to act from the road down the centre of the village to the left & Irah from the right from the road. Nelson advanced in close support to mop up the village. Our objective was reached by 6.30 a.m. We dug in I.M.G. yards beyond Sunken Road from C.25.D.64 — C.25.F.8.9. Our front was held by C.B. & Coys from left to right with A Coy in reserve in the Sunken Rd. Roughly 21 prisoners from 81st & 2nd I.R. were taken by the Batt. The day was spent in improving the position during the afternoon bodies of the enemy in retirement were observed crossing over the crest between OPPY & FRESNES-LES-MONTAUBAN. I.R.H.F.	
"	24.4.17	3 p.m.	The Germans made a strong counter attack at 3 p.m. & were completely refused by our barrage & rifle fire. The Germans suffered very heavily. I.R.H.F.	

Arab Batt.

WAR DIARY

Summary of Events & Information

PLACE	DATE	HOUR	
ST CATHERINE	23-4-17	4 AM	Relieved by Kew. Battn., marched back to bivouac at St Catherine. P.R.W.T.
MAROEUIL	"	3 PM	marched to billets at Maroeuil arriving at 5 p.m. Total number of casualties sustained during operation.
			Officers Killed 1, Died of Wounds 0, Wounded 1, Missing 0, Total 10
			Men 4 / 23 / 232 / 36 / 293
			303 P.R.W.T.
"	26-4-17		Day spent in cleaning up. Corps Commander congratulated C.O. on it Battalion. Greetings received from II ANZAC Corps on anniversary of landing at Gallipoli. P.R.W.T.
FREVILLERS	27-4-17		Battn. left Maroeuil, marched to billets at Frevillers arriving 6.30 p.m. P.R.W.T.
	28-4-17	1.15 PM	
MAGNICOURT	29-4-17	11.0 AM	Battn. moved into billets at Magnicourt arriving 12 noon. P.R.W.T.
"	30-4-17		Day spent in clearing up; all H. Batt. had a bath. P.R.W.T.

Mendolssennet
Lt Colonel
Commanding

SECRET.   DRAKE BATTALION ORDER No 3.

Ref. POINT DU JOUR 1/10,000.

1. **INFORMATION.** Enemy is reported to be holding GAVRELLE-OPPY Line and GAVRELLE village with a trench garrison & machine guns.

2. **INTENTION.** GAVRELLE-OPPY Line and GAVRELLE Village will be attacked in accordance with Brigade order No.G.238.

3. **INSTRUCTIONS.** Formation and allotment of objectives.

   Formations. B Coy. on right, D Coy. on left, in first and second waves (waves 20x apart) C Coy. less 2 platoons in third wave (50x behind 2nd wave) A Coy less 4 sections in 4th wave (50x behind 3rd wave) 2 Platoons C.Coy less 2 sections, in reserve (50x behind 4th wave)

   Moppers up. Four sections A.Coy. in line 6x in rear of first wave. Two sections C.Coy in line 6x in rear of left of 2nd wave.

   Lewis Guns. Lewis guns attached to platoons in first wave will be on flanks of second wave, Lewis Gunners will be in file.

   Bombers. Bombers and rifle grenadiers will be used as situations arise and conform to the general alignment.

   Allotment of objectives. B. and D. Coys will capture and consolidate third German trench leaving A.Coys Moppers up in first German trench and C.Coys Moppers up in second German trench C.Coy occupy and consolidate second German trench A.Coy occupy and consolidate first German trench.

   Limits.
   B.Coy   H.6.b.9.6. to B.30.d.3.3.
   D.Coy   B.30.d.3.3. to B.30.d.2.8.
   C.Coy.(2 platoons) B.30.c.7½.2½. to B.30.c.6.7½.
   A.Coy.   H.6.a.4.5. to B.30.c.3½.7½.

(x) In the event of :-
   (a) The Battalion being required to move up to fifth objective (Brigade order para 3. sub.para e.) Battalion will continue to advance in above order and 2 platoons of C.Coy in reserve will move up to the alignment of second German trench. In this case the rifle grenadiers and Bombers will be in front of the waves, and advance down the streets of the village engaging any Machine Guns. The waves in rear will keep the general alignment as much as possible through the village and reorganise on the road on the eastern side of the village before passing through the HOOD BATTN to fifth objective
   (b)(If fourth objective final objective One
   The Battalion being detailed to finish the mopping up of the village and helping the Hood Battn to consolidate the fourth objective. Battalion will mop up systematically as shown on Map A. and move up to the HOOD BATTN to help in consolidation.
   A continuation of these orders is being prepared regarding Battalion communications, Battle equipment, Dumps etc.

                                        Commandr, Commanding Drake Battn

SECRET.   189th Infantry Brigade No.G.236 (copy)

1. **Troops employed.** (a) The attack will be carried out by the DRAKE
    BATTALION on the right and the NELSON BATTALION on the left.
    The HOOD BATTALION will be in close support and the HAWKE BATTALION
    in reserve.
    (b) Eight guns of the 189th Machine Gun Company will be employed.
    (c) Four guns of the 189th S.B. Battery will be sent forward and
        four will be held in reserve.
    (d) A portion of the 248th Field Company R.E. will be utilised
        to make strong points on the eastern outskirts of GAVRELLE.

2. **BOUNDARIES.**
    The dividing line between Battalions will be as laid down in
    Brigade Order No.85 and will be continued from C.23.Central to
    C.23 Central.

3. **OBJECTIVE.** (a) The first Brigade and Divisional objective will be
    FRIGID trench running from H.6.b.95.66. to the
    GAVRELLE-ARRAS road and thence a line across to the
    junction of FRISKY and FILMY trenches.

    (b) The second Brigade objective will be the road running
        from I.1.a.15.70. to B.30.b.3.6.

    (c) The third Brigade objective will be the road running
        from I.1.b.05.85.to C.25.a.2.8.

    (d) The fourth Brigade and second Divisional objective
        will be a line adapted to the lie of the country
        about 390 yards in front of the third objective.

    (e) The fifth Brigade and the third Divisional objective
        will be a line from C.26.c.7.0. to C.25.c.0.6.

        This final objective would enable patrols to be pushed
        on to SQUARE WOOD and HOLLOW COPSE.
        would bring all the assaulting troops clear of the
        village and would conform to the general movement
        of troops on our flanks.

4. **METHOD OF ATTACK.**
    (a) The first objective would be attacked by the DRAKE
        and NELSON BATTALIONS in four waves of platoons in
        depth, the first and second waves going on to the
        objective, the third staying in the second German line,
        & the fourth remaining in the first German line.
    (b) The HOOD BATTALION would then attack the second,
        third and fourth objectives in two waves, pausing at
        the second and third for eight minutes and consolidating
        the fourth objective as a support line to the final
        objective.
        They will be followed by the DRAKE and NELSON BATTNS
        in four waves, the leading wave being 150 yards in
        rear of the Hood Battalion's second wave
        These Battalions will do any more mopping up in the
        village which might be necessary.
    (c) Drake and Nelson Battalions will close up to the
        protective barrage and when it lifts they will advance
        to the fifth objective, which they will consolidate.

2.

          (d) If the fifth objective is considered to be too far east for the line, one of these Battalions will be sent forward to assist the Hood Battn to to consolidate on the fourth objective which will thus become the final objective. The other Battalion will hold the old German front line system.

5. BARRAGE. (a) The 18pdr. shrapnel barrage will open 100 yards in front of the German wire and will creep at the rate of 100 yards every four minutes to the first objective, it will stay 200 yards in front of it for 34 minutes, it will then creep to 200 yards beyond the second objective where it will stay for eight minutes, similarly it will creep to 200 yards beyond the third objective and stay for eight minutes. It will move from there at zero plus 90 minutes to the final objective

          (b) The heavy artillery barrage will be placed in front of the shrapnel barrage.

          (c) A machine gun barrage will be placed 300 yards in front of the shrapnel barrage under arrangements to be made by Corps Machine Gun Officer.

6. ASSEMBLY. (a) The assaulting Battalions will move up to the tranchee de depart which is being dug 250 yards from the German wire on Y/Z night and form up with their leading wave in front of the trench, their second wave in the trench, and their third and fourth waves in rear of it.

          (b) The Hood Battn will be formed up in our existing front line some 400 yards in rear.

          (c) The Hawke Battn will be utilised for carrying parties and the remainder will be accommodated on the line of the BAILLEUL-FAMPOUX road.

          (d) A battalion of the 188th Brigade will be at the disposal of the G.O.C. 188th Brigade and will be in reserve in the POINT DU JOUR-FARBUS line.

7. LOCATION OF HEADQUARTERS.

	Brigade.	H.3.d.4.9.
	Right group) Divl. Artilly)	H.3.b.7.2.
	Advanced report) centre.)	B.28.d.6.5.
	Drake Battn) Nelson Battn)	In the assembly trenches.
	Hood Battn)	In the present front line.
	Hawke Battn)	H.3.a.0.2.
	M.G.Coy.)	H.4.b.95.30.
	S.M.Batty)	B.28.d.5.8.

8. ADMINISTRATIVE ARRANGEMENTS.
    The preliminary administrative arrangements will be the subject of a separate memorandum.

9. SIGNAL COMMUNICATIONS. The Brigade Signal Officer will issue a memorandum on signal communications during the attack after consultation with the Officer Commanding 63rd R.N. Divl. Signal Company.

signed R.W. Barnett
Capt
Brigade Major

2.

5.	Brigade Orders.	Particular attention is to be paid to para 20.
6.	Stragglers.	No stragglers are to be tolerated.
7.	"Retire".	There is no command "Retire".
8.	Flanks.	If the flanks are held up push on. This will help all concerned.
9.	Barrage.	Keep close to the barrage.

Commander, R.N.V.R.,

Commanding "Drake" Battalion.

Not to be taken into action.

S E C R E T.

DRAKE BATTALION ORDER NO. 4.

1. **Information.** Enemy is reported to as holding the GAVRELLE-OPPY line and the GAVRELLE village with a normal trench garrison and machine guns.

2. **Intention.** The GAVRELLE-OPPY line and GAVRELLE village will be attacked in accordance with Brigade Order No. 86 (and amendments).

3. **Instructions.** (a) **Formations.**

   63rd. Divisional Standard System of Attack.

   Waves.

   First and second waves "B" Company, Right.
   "D" Company, Left.

   Moppers-up.

   Four sections "A" Company, four sections "C" Company.

   Third wave. "C" Company.

   Fourth wave. "A" Company.

   Lewis Guns. Lewis gunners in file and disposed as situations arise.

   Bombers. Bombers and rifle grenadiers will be used as situations arise and conform to general alignment.

   (b) **Allotment of objectives and Company Boundaries.**

   Boundaries. Left of "D" Company Battalion Left Boundary. Right of "B" Company, Battalion Right boundary.
   Dividing line. B. 30.c.5½.1. to B.30.c.7.1. to B.30.d.8½.1. to C.25.c.1.2½. to C.25.d.1.4½.

   Objectives. Whole Battalion will move forward in the Divisional Attack formation until final objective is reached.
   First wave will leave "A" Company's moppers-up in first German trench.
   Second wave will leave "C" Company's moppers--up in second German trench.
   These moppers-up will be brought forward when their work is finished and all remaining mopping-up will be done by waves concerned.

4. **Consolidation.** On reaching GREEN line consolidation will be carried on as rapidly as possible. A traversed trench is to be made. The quickest method of making this trench: line up the Company, tell off in fours, every other section of fours to take six paces to the rear and then the whole line dig in.

Army Form C. 2118.

Drake Bn

WAR DIARY
or
INTELLIGENCE SUMMARY. 10th L.B.
(Erase heading not required.)

Instructions regarding War Diaries and Intelligence Summaries are contained in F. S. Regs., Part II. and the Staff Manual respectively. Title pages will be prepared in manuscript.

Place	Date	Hour	Summary of Events and Information	Remarks and references to Appendices
MAGNICOURT	1-5-17 to 3-5-17		These three days were devoted to Platoon, Company and Battalion Training.	10 h.L.B.
" ROCLINCOURT	4-5-17		Lieut+ Q.M. J. SAUNDERS joined Battalion for duty as Quartermaster on the 28 Febr. D.R.O 2143 D.h.L.B. Battalion left MAGNICOURT at 11 a.m. and marched to TINQUES, thence by motor bus to G.6.a (MAP 51.B) where they encamped in bivouacs.	10.h.L.B.
"	5-5-17 to 19-5-17		The whole battalion employed by night, in constructing a new RESERVE LINE — known as the RED LINE — between the POINT DUR JOUR — FARBUS LINE and the GAVRELLE — OPPY LINE. MAP REFERENCE. MAP 51 B NW. — B.28.B.71. & H.5.C.8.7. 10 h.L.B. Total Casualties during this period were Killed, one O.R. Died of wounds, one O.R. Wounded, five O.R.s. The following officers joined the battalion on May 4, 1917. Lt. JAMES WILFRED TURRELL, Lt. JOHN HEDLEY GALLIER LILLYWHITE, Sub.Lt. EDWARD AUBREY JENKINS, Sub.Lt. SIDNEY GEORGE WALKER. D.h.L.B.	
St CATHERINE	20-5-17	2:45 p.m.	Battalion moved to tents at G9.c. D.h.L.B.	
"	21-5-17 to 31-5-17		Battalion employed in constructing new communication trench at H.5.C.4.9 & H.4.D.2.3 during this period. Casualties one O.R. wounded 10 h.L.B.	[MAP 51 B. N.W.]

Commander R.N.V.R.
Commanding DRAKE Bn.

WAR DIARY
or
INTELLIGENCE SUMMARY.
(Erase heading not required.)

Army Form C. 2118.

Vol / 2
Drake Battn

Place	Date	Hour	Summary of Events and Information	Remarks and references to Appendices
St Catherine	1/6/17		189th Brigade relieved the 190th Inf Brigade from WINDMILL the night of Gavrelle to OPPY WOOD. DRAKE BATTN in reserve.	No/p 51B. NW
		2 pm	Relieved 10th R.D. Fs. from H.1.b.3.8. to B.26.C.1.4. Relief complete 4.30 p.m. @	
Gavrelle	2/6/17		2 Companies employed by night improving front line system of trenches	
	3/6/17		Same. Rev. W.J. Dowling & Lieut "Q.M" Wilson joined Battalion. One casualty.	
	4/6/17		Same. Sgt. Lt. Penrod. D. Coy wounded.	
Gavrelle	5/6/17		Battalion relieved. Stood to from WINDMILL to the aeroplane in 1,000" N of Gavrelle. Four casualties.	
	6/6/17		Our own artillery very active & several enemy planes caught up by our Machine & Lewis Gun fire. 3 wounded.	
	7/6/17		Rather quiet day except for spasmodic bursts by our artillery & nothing of moment. SSM 2 killed from the enemy. Lieut Aitken wounded.	
	8/6/17		3 wounded. Enemy fairly active but no casualties	

WAR DIARY or INTELLIGENCE SUMMARY

Army Form C. 2118.

Drake Battn

Place	Date	Hour	Summary of Events and Information	Remarks and references to Appendices
Gavrelle	9/6/17		Our artillery very active co-operating with machine guns. One casualty from our own artillery	
	10/6/17	3/4 pm	Battalion relieved by 14th Y & L Regt. We marched back to St Nicholas at Rothincourt — no casualties	
	11/6/17		Improving billets & cleaning up	
Rothincourt	12/6/17	10 pm	Improving billets. Lewis Gun army N.J. Bouffal	
	13/6/17		do	
	14/6/17			
	15/6/17		Left Roclincourt. saw C.W. to new Thanes Trench & old German Support Rly	
	16/6/17			
	17/6/17			
	19/6/17		Working parties by night	
	20/6/17		Relieved 2nd R.M.L.I. in trenches at Maarne	
	21/6/17			
	22/6/17			
	23/6/17			
Maarne	27/6/17		4 days course of training. Sent to Battn on Bombing L. Gun P.T. Musketry	
	28/6/17		Demonstrations by two platoons before all officers of 189 Bde in open fighting & trench storming	
	29/6/17 3/7/17		Training	
			About Totals	

Army Form C. 2118.

Drake Bn Vol/13

WAR DIARY
or
INTELLIGENCE SUMMARY.
(Erase heading not required.)

Instructions regarding War Diaries and Intelligence Summaries are contained in F. S. Regs., Part II. and the Staff Manual respectively. Title pages will be prepared in manuscript.

Place	Date	Hour	Summary of Events and Information	Remarks and references to Appendices
Church Brade	1.7.17.		E.A.J.	
	2.7.17.		Brigade Day. Training in open warfare. Men were fitted up in the afternoon. E.A.J.	
	3.7.17		Inspection of whole Battalion by C.O. including transport etc. Training in ceremonial drill during the morning + march past of a battalion	
	4.7.17.		Companies in line. 63rd R.N.D. Battalion left Maroeuil Wakefield Camp. Poclincourt. (A.28 O6.3)	
	5.7.17		Training by Divisional Rifle Coy.	
	6.7.17	10.30 a.m.	Battalion inspected in Horse Shew Ground (A26 a 7-6) by Army Commander (2nd Army) General Sir H.S. Horne K.C.B.	
	7.7.17		Training and ceremonial drill in preparation for His Majesty the King's Inspection. RB	
	8.7.17			
	9.7.17			
	10.7.17.	11.00 AM	His Majesty the King inspected the Drake Battalion	
	11.7.17		together with the Anson, Hawke, PP.R.O. (A26 O6-6) RB	
	12.7.17		by Batn from wh. the Brigade is formed at inspection.	
			Infantry Brigade, 63rd (R.N) Division. —	

Place	Date	Hour	Summary of Events and Information	Remarks and references to Appendices
	12.4.17		Continued. O.C. "D" Coy. & Batalion. The Divisional Commander telephoned me personally to say that he was very pleased with the opinion of the great success of the raid given by H.M. the KING – The Batalion was relieved on the night 63rd – 64th Lanes evening, and the prisoners were sent to the (6.N.) Division. Three coming to see me next morning stated to me. The effort to make the raid a success. I could not have given more credit and Thanks. Pat H.N. and one [?] who attended to prisoners were much struck with the bright appearance the men made inspite of the great exertion of the raid. Sgt of Battalion ordered to have Lt. & my Company Sergt Major [?] General bonus G. 18.9. Sept. Brigade A. & R. 11/4/17. H.H.R.	
		11 am	OPPY TRENCH was shown with sigs by No. 721 Artillery. Machine gun was firing from a point in OPPY VILLAGE (C.13.A.b.4) Enemy firing 6.12 Quite hostile aeroplanes over our lines (L.18.A.b.m.14/26.3.6).	
		11.30		
		6.30 pm	in & were close by but by no means extensive. Patrols were out during the night. 1 Officer and 20 other ORs (B.18.d.6.0) getting close to enemy wire. Relieve in S.E. of OPPY WOOD and located [?] machine gun at (C.13.A.6.4) Weather FAIR. Wind light weather westerly. N.A.	

Army Form C. 2118.

WAR DIARY
or
INTELLIGENCE SUMMARY.
(Erase heading not required.)

Instructions regarding War Diaries and Intelligence Summaries are contained in F. S. Regs., Part II. and the Staff Manual respectively. Title pages will be prepared in manuscript.

Place	Date	Hour	Summary of Events and Information	Remarks and references to Appendices
	12.7.17		The enemy shelled OPPY TRENCH (B18. c.2. 8). Nothing the night quietly. shelled EARL TRENCH with only 4 range. Machine guns [illegible] active. [illegible] guns new active during night. [illegible]/7/17 Enemy guns were and [illegible] - Trench shorter his Battery Uniit at (C.13. a8.7.5) his active to enemy T.M.s. Enemy gun coming [illegible] on OPPY WOOD on our front to enemy fines (0.13.a) 9a to B.18. a.55) Aeroplanes of both sides fairly active during evening. Patrols [illegible] and Enemy patrol [illegible] in OPPY WOOD to our front. [illegible] the [illegible] shortly [illegible] our front. No.1 [illegible] [illegible] enemy artillery was active but became long long. N.Co'D SUPPORT TRENCH + surroundings - hit by enemy [illegible] [illegible] weather.	
	14/7/17		Our casualties. [illegible] pnte.1 pnte.1 Sgt. No. [illegible] enemy patrol [illegible] our lines during the night. [illegible] a bird of L/Cpl [illegible] B/4. No.3 Pat about 10.30 p.m. [illegible]. Patrols lay along N.15 B.57. OPPY WOOD nothing to [illegible] Enemy a/plane shot N.1 B.55 [illegible]. FAIR. hostile [illegible] Wind S.W. Nile.	
	15/7/17		Situation [illegible] [illegible] [illegible] burning of British rifle new attack to the Duke Batt for instruction of [illegible] [illegible] during to early Lineman [illegible] and a part of the [illegible] to cover [illegible] to [illegible] our [illegible] at B.51.6. 16 [illegible] Batt to [illegible]	

WAR DIARY
or
INTELLIGENCE SUMMARY

Army Form C. 2118.

Place	Date	Hour	Summary of Events and Information	Remarks and references to Appendices
	July 16/17	9.0 a.m.	Situation quiet. A party of Welsh Rifles relieved party of "Welsh Bosp" Rifles who were attached to the Battn. At 9.30 pm Hood Bn relieved our A.D. & B. Platoons of 6 Coys in the line [illegible]. Were Battn now in Brass Casualties.	
		11 p.m.	1 Platoon of B. Coy at 11 p.m. went back to a position in REDLINE (B.D., S.S.O.) [illegible]	
	July 17		Situation quiet. A.A. and B. Coys moving in REDLINE, tying up shelters for Coy H.Q. also filled in ammo. Several Hostile aeroplane and an air ravish the hut. A large field of front [illegible] crossed the German lines spent 15 min being shot at [illegible] Line (5) Casualties. Carrying Party digging trench in VISCOUNT TRENCH. no hostile [illegible]. Trench run from N. CADORNA TRENCH to E. CAIRO TRENCH. [signed]	
	July 18		Situation quiet. Weather mixed. Sunlit Sw [illegible] Carrying on same work as last night. Digging trench from N. CADORNA TRENCH to E. CAIRO TRENCH. One (1) Casualty. [signed]	
	July 19		Situation quiet. Weather changeable. Comp. I/O. No working party last night. Next [illegible] 188 [illegible] Coy carry up to 4000 S.A.A. Ammn Bombs and [illegible] inform [illegible] to REDLINE. [signed]	
	July 20		Situation quiet. [illegible] entertaining in RED LINE. [signed]	
	July 21		Situation quiet. Weather [illegible] for [illegible] W. Working out at night finishing trench in front of CADORNA TRENCH. During the day Companies were improving their shelters and trench. [signed]	

Army Form C. 2118.

WAR DIARY
or
INTELLIGENCE SUMMARY.
(Erase heading not required.)

Instructions regarding War Diaries and Intelligence Summaries are contained in F. S. Regs., Part II. and the Staff Manual respectively. Title pages will be prepared in manuscript.

Place	Date	Hour	Summary of Events and Information	Remarks and references to Appendices
	July 22 1917		Location Hull. Drake Bath relieved at this by 1st/4th Royal Sussex Regiment. Bn. entrained for Hull and proceeded to BEVERLEY CAMP. at G4d.	
	July 23		Whole of day was given up to cleaning of gear and reorganisation. At 2 o'clock there was a Battalion parade in which all gear was thoroughly inspected.	
	July 24		Training in Platoon drill by Platoon Commanders, Physical Training, Bayonet Fighting, mechanism of and lecture on Lewis Guns, Musketry and Bombing.	
	July 25		Training as above. One "O.R." accidentally wounded.	
	July 26		Training as above. 2nd/Lieut WALKER J.W.S. and 1 O.R. accidentally wounded.	
	July 27		Training as above and Coys. operating in darkness, wearing respirators and advancing in artillery formation and moving forward in issue R.E.	
	July 28		Battalion sports.	
	July 29		Chief Parade - Wet day.	
	July 30		Regimental Footer. Relieved Howe Bn. in right subsector of East sector.	

Commanding

A7092. Wt. W12839/M1294. 750,000. 1/17. D, D & L., Ltd. Forms/C2118/12.

Army Form C. 2118.

WAR DIARY
or
INTELLIGENCE SUMMARY.
(Erase heading not required)

Instructions regarding War Diaries and Intelligence Summaries are contained in F. S. Regs., Part II. and the Staff Manual respectively. Title pages will be prepared in manuscript.

Place	Date	Hour	Summary of Events and Information	Remarks and references to Appendices
	July 31		Artillery (Enemy) Very slight shelling of WINDE and WINDE SUPPORT Trenches.	
			Our Own: Quiet.	
			Trench Mortars. Early this morning enemy mortars fired on O.25 a/f from WIDE TR.	
			Aerial Activity. One of our planes flew very low over CAMERA TR. firing his guns in our trench.	
			Enemy Retaliation: One recorded at 11 am and again at 12.15 from direction of VITRY.	
			Visibility: Very indifferent in early morning, clearing slightly as day went on but getting very hazy again in afternoon. In evening even new objects were obscured by heavy haze over hills.	
			Enemy Snipers: Fairly active overnight firing chiefly on WINDE SUPPORT from direction of WINDMILL TR.	
			WIND. Early morning, hardly felt. In afternoon 5 m.p.h. N.N.E. Col. of evening slight rainfall continuing throughout greater part of night.	
			MACHINE GUNS. Enemys - Intermittent tapping fire two positions all along front. Very active against aircraft all day from WINDMILL TR. Our Own: Keeping up steady harassing fire throughout night. [signature]	

A9093). Wt. W118591/M1250. 750,000. 1/17. D.D & L., Ltd. Forms/C218/8/4.

WAR DIARY or INTELLIGENCE SUMMARY

Army Form C. 2118.

Drake Bn

Vol 14

Date	Hour	Summary of Events and Information	Remarks and references to Appendices
Aug 2		Situation much as day before with an exception to SSW. Situated front line SSW. Gittes & entire left Coy together to 604.	
3		Reported that an enemy patrol from Rails surprised & destroyed a Lewis Gun and crew in 604	
4		of 1 a.m. heavy T.M. action against Gittes, being shelled enemy will & hornets enemy artillery shelling night & day with shells S.OS., bombs	
5		were sent over at 2 am & Enemy artillery very active & intermittent at 2am. Gittes. Enemy Concentrated on trench junction Konton Pond. Aircraft both enemy & own very active	
6		Situation quiet. Battalion relieved by Anson Batt & moved to Boreham in RED LINE (B.T.S.O) HW	
7		In RED LINE. Working parties digging new cable trench. Reinforcing existing trenches. Casualties 2nd Lieut PARNELL & SW3 lieut Le Souleur Killed. 10T wounded. Relieved evening of 6th by 4th Batt Royal Fusiliers & moved back to BEVERLY CAMP at G.4.0. HW	
8-16		Reorganization & General Clearing up. Programme	

18/9

WAR DIARY
or
INTELLIGENCE SUMMARY.
(Erase heading not required.)

Army Form C. 2118.

Place	Date	Hour	Summary of Events and Information	Remarks and references to Appendices
	Aug 20/1/17		Raining all day. Programme 63Hb	
	21/1/17		Ditto 63Hb	
	22/1/17		Ditto 63Hb	
	23/1/17		63Hb. Brigade Sports. DESERTED CAMP. 63Hb	
	24/1/17		Ditto. Relieved HOWE Bn in R.I. Trench 63Hb	
			63Hb	
	25/1/17		End weather, situation quiet. 63Hb	
			End weather. Situation quiet. Four Casualties (2 killed, 2 wounded) Genuine 63Hb	
	26/1/17		Raining. Observation poor. Situation quiet. 63Hb	
	27/1/17		Shot weather, observation fair, situation quiet. Our artillery active during the day. 122 Reinforcement from Battn. 63Hb	
	28/1/17		B C + D Companies being in the NO MAN'S LAND in NAVAL TRENCH. 63Hb	
			Day relieved NELSON Bn. 63Hb	
	29/1/17		Cloudy, observation fair, situation normal. Whole Battalion carrying 63Hb	
	30/1/17		Cloudy, observation poor, situation normal, carrying out. 63Hb	
	31/1/17		Fine, rain at intervals. Battalion carrying (Comms. Relief) 63Hb	Wm B. Beak Lieut. to OC DRAKE Bn

30th. September, 1917.

WAR DIARY

of

DRAKE BATTALION.
189th. Infantry Brigade.

From

1st. SEPTEMBER, 1917

to

30th. SEPTEMBER, 1917.

D.A.G.,
   A.G'S OFFICE,
      BASE.

WAR DIARY or **INTELLIGENCE SUMMARY**

Army Form C. 2118.

(Erase heading not required.)

Place	Date	Hour	Summary of Events and Information	Remarks and references to Appendices
	Sept 1.		Battalion quiet. Officers writing letters with the Officers of the ANSON BN. DRAKE Battalion relieved Bn in TRENCH AND SUPPORT LINE.	
	2.		Started quiet. Sent for Lieut. Drake who returned by 2nd R.M.L.I. offrs	
	3.		Training. Whole down in Battalion programme.	
	4.		Battalion programme offrs.	
	5.		Training & lect down in offrs.	
	6.		Ditto	
	7.		Ditto	
	8.		Ditto	
	9.		Church Parade. Church service by Revd Chapman. Found of Army officiating. Acting Commandant present officers present offrs Church Parade Coy Commanders advised troops. Prepared to have to move trench in Railway CUTTING. Relieved the trenches at 3 p.m. att	
	10.			

Army Form C. 2118.

WAR DIARY
or
INTELLIGENCE SUMMARY.
(Erase heading not required.)

Instructions regarding War Diaries and Intelligence Summaries are contained in F. S. Regs., Part II. and the Staff Manual respectively. Title pages will be prepared in manuscript.

Place	Date	Hour	Summary of Events and Information	Remarks and references to Appendices
Sept 10/17			Attached 90th Brigade for working party with 6th	
	11.		R. Battalion improved during the morning in afternoon two companies on working party, two on cable burying two on Bailleul Bog – 15th Bn	
	12		Same as 11/9/17. 15th Bn	
	13		Ditto 15th Bn	
	14		Weather fine. Same as 13/9/17. 15th Bn	
	15		Ditto	
	16		Relieved Norm Bn in R. his res. Company were prov. interior high during of their heavy T.M. fire off at TCHAD TRENCH. (Scene of that evening) 15th Bn	
	17		Quiet day. Wind SSW	
	18		Weather good. Situation normal. Enemy T.M. shld CHAD TRENCH	
	19		Weather fine. Wind SW situation good. 15th Bn	
	20		Trenches normal. Wind W. situation quiet. 15th Bn	
	21		Weather normal. Wind SW Companies during evening carried out reliefs	

WAR DIARY
or
INTELLIGENCE SUMMARY

Army Form C. 2118.

Place	Date	Hour	Summary of Events and Information	Remarks and references to Appendices
Sept. 22			Situation quiet throughout. Artillery sniper active. Rain during night. T.M. & M.G. fire quiet.	
" 23			Enemy (SW) Garrison normal. WXD	
" 24			Front line circular quiet. WXD	
" 25			Garrison relieved at 1.30 pm by 1/5 London Regt. CSRE. Battalion moved to TINCOURT and 1/8 Lon WXD	
" 26			Battalion cleaning up, and reorganising WXD	
" 27			Trained — for program WXD	WXD 6 5 grenzlowers and umbrellas
" 28			" "	WXD 6
" 29			" "	WXD 6
" 30			Church Parade, and presentation of R.W.R (L.S.) medal to C.P.O. A/Sgt Larcock 1/5 Ln. R.	WXD 6

Munderbenman
Lieut Col R.M.R.
Commanding 1/5 th Battalion

WAR DIARY or INTELLIGENCE SUMMARY

Army Form C. 2118

4th Bn Royal Warwickshire Regt
4 OC 16

Place	Date	Hour	Summary of Events and Information	Remarks and references to Appendices
Fr. 901 TINQUES	1/10/17		Training. Battalion R.H.Q. Battalion marched to Sav'y	
	2/10/17		entrained and left France for Belgium.	
Wed	3/10/17		Arrived Proven, marched to Billets near HERZELLE. 10th W. 8th W.	
	4/10/17		Training.	
	5/10/17		Left HERZELLE by bus at 11.am. 10th W.	
	6/10/17		DINGHE arriving 1.15 pm. 10th W.	
			Left DIRTY BUCKET CAMP 10th W. ↑ DIRTY BUCKET CAMP - ELVER-	
	7/10/17		arriving at 5.15 p.m. 10th W. ↑ REIGERSBURG CAMP, NEAR YPRES. 10th W.	
			Battalion working party of 500 men working on R CHT	
	8/10/17		RAILWAY near ESSEX Fm, new YSER CANAL 10th W.	
			Battalion standing by for working parties. Training. 10th W.	
	9/10/17		Working party of 250 men employed with 1 C.R.T. 10th W.	
			200 men standing by for working parties. 10th W.	
	10/10/17		250 men employed with 1 C.R.T. 2 OR wounded 10th W.	
	11/10/17		500 men employed with 1 C.R.T. 10th W.	
			Casualties. 1 OR Died of Wounds. 4 OR Wounded	

A 50931. Wt. W1289/M1298. 750,000. 1/17. D. D. & L. Ltd. Forms/C2118/24.

Army Form C. 2118.

WAR DIARY
or
INTELLIGENCE SUMMARY.
(Erase heading not required.)

Instructions regarding War Diaries and Intelligence Summaries are contained in F. S. Regs., Part II. and the Staff Manual respectively. Title pages will be prepared in manuscript.

Place	Date	Hour	Summary of Events and Information	Remarks and references to Appendices
In the Field	12/10/17		650 men on railway work with 7th C.R.T. #C.R.B	
"	13/10/17		2. 750 men employed with 7th C.R.T. #C.R.B – 168 men and 9 horses 20 C.R.T, 108 Dog wds	
"	14/10/17		250 men employed with 7th C.R.T. #C.R.B	
"	15/10/17		750 men employed with 7th C.R.T. #C.R.B	
"	16/10/17		650 men employed with 7th C.R.T. #C.R.B	
"	17/10/17		men employed with 7th C.R.T. #C.R.B	
"	18/10/17		men employed with 7th C.R.T. #C.R.B	
"	19/10/17		One Officer, 1 P.O. and 50 O.Rs. working at HOSPITAL SPUR, ST JULIEN opening line at 6am ft. Four Officers, 5 P.Os. and 200 O.Rs. NORDHOF YARD at 7.15 am ft. Two Parties – One of 1 N.C.O. and 25 O.Rs. at 6am; the other of 1 P.O. and 250 O.Rs. at 12 noon – ft. Parties at NORTHUMBERLAND YARD. ft Two Parties: 1 Officer, 1 P.O. and 50 O.Rs. at 6am 1 Officer, 1 P.O. and 50 O.Rs. at 12 noon } BOCHE CASTLE LOOP ft One Officer, 1 P.O., 50 O.Rs. C.R.T. AGADIR CAMP, at 7am. — BAND: 1 P.O. 200 O.Rs. C.R.T. Gravel at 8am. ft (loading sandbags). H.P. Dolton Major R.E.	

WAR DIARY
or
INTELLIGENCE SUMMARY.
(Erase heading not required.)

Army Form C. 2118.

Place	Date	Hour	Summary of Events and Information	Remarks and references to Appendices
Æcia	2/10/17	200	men on railway work under 7 R.R.T.	ℍℍℍ
FLD	21/10	300	" on railway work	7 C.R.T. ℍℍℍ
	22/10/17	400	" " " "	7 C.R.T ℍℍℍ
	23	600	" on railway work	7 C.R.T ℍℍℍ
	24	4 Officers and 92 o.r. paraded a XVIII Corps Hill for orders. Action.		ℍℍℍ
		550	men on railway work	7 C.R.T. Casualties 2 o.r killed, 2 o.r wounded. 2 o.r sick. ℍℍℍ
	26	350	" on railway work	7 C.R.T. Sub/Lt. S.E. Briddon wnd + Sick and 1 or Sick ℍℍℍ
	27	500	" on railway work	7 C.R.T ℍℍℍ
	28	500	" Tramway "	7 C.R.T ℍℍℍ
	29	450	" on Railway "	7 C.R.T ℍℍℍ
		Working Parties Nil.— Brigadier Gen Phillips inspected the Battalion		
	30/10/17	Training. Supplied a party of 1 Officer and 50 o.r as Stretcher bearers — Casualties — One Killed, and 8 o.r wounded.		ℍℍℍ
	30/10/17	Training. Supplied a party of 6 officers and 250 o.r as Stretcher Bearers. On account of 190th Bde operations. Casualties.		ℍℍℍ
	31/10/17	Battalion moved forward to CHEDDAR VILLA & IRISH FARM in support. 1 Killed 3 o.r wounded 8 o.r. Missing 1 O.R.		ℍℍℍ H.R Dowart Lt Col

Army Form C. 2118.

189/3 Drake Bn Vol 17

WAR DIARY
or
INTELLIGENCE SUMMARY.
(Erase heading not required.)

Instructions regarding War Diaries and Intelligence Summaries are contained in F. S. Regs., Part II. and the Staff Manual respectively. Title pages will be prepared in manuscript.

Place	Date	Hour	Summary of Events and Information	Remarks and references to Appendices
	1/11/17.		In support to HAWKE & NELSON Battns at CHEDDAR VILLA. LEFT CHEDDAR VILLA. 200 min employed carrying ammunition returns to front line.	
	2/11/17.		LEFT IRISH FARM for left subsector of Divisional Front. "B" Coy left at IRISH FARM training for minor operation. 1 OR wounded.	
	3/11/17.		In front line. Heavy barrage on BANFF HOUSE about 2 p.m. lasting until 4.30 p.m. At 9.00 p.m. on this date two Coys carried out a minor operation and captured SOURD FARM, advancing our line about 200 yards. 1 officer & 3 ORs were taken prisoner. 2 killed 3 ORs wounded.	
	4/11/17.		In front line. Our own artillery active rest part of day. BANFF HOUSE was heavily shelled during the day. Commander W Wernicke Bennett M.O. severely wounded. Lieut. A. Harty wounded. "B" Coy carried out a minor operation against enemy posts in conjunction with one platoon of HOOD BATTN, advancing our line about 100 yds towards TOURNANT FARM. 3 Machine Guns were captured. BURNS HOUSE Lens new runs V.28.a.6.2. to SOURD FARM - V.27.B.4.9. - V.27.a.30.95. (SPRIET MAP). 4 ORs killed, 15 ORs wounded, 2 ORs missing HQ Drake Bn Cr Cmdr	

WAR DIARY
or
INTELLIGENCE SUMMARY.

Army Form C. 2118.

(Erase heading not required.)

Instructions regarding War Diaries and Intelligence Summaries are contained in F. S. Regs., Part II. and the Staff Manual respectively. Title pages will be prepared in manuscript.

Place	Date	Hour	Summary of Events and Information	Remarks and references to Appendices
	5/11/17		In front line. Intermittent shelling during day. Heavy Bosche barrage behind BANFF HOUSE about 5.30 pm. Relieved by composite Coys of 188th Brigade. After relief proceed to IRISH FARM.	
	6/11/17		Left IRISH FARM about 10. am for R.& D CAMP (F. X. d. 1.4) arriving there about 6.00pm.	
	7/11/17		Cleaning up & reorganisation. Commander W. STEERNDALE BENNETT also died of wounds at 62nd C.C.S.	
	8/11/17 9/11/17		do. Training.	
			The Funeral of Commander W. STEERNDALE BENNETT also took place from 62nd CCS to DOZINGHEM CEMETERY. It was attended by the Divisional General, Members of Divisional & Brigade Staffs, Battalion Commanders of 189th Brigade, & 15 Offr. 7/20 men representing DRAKE BATTALION. He was buried with full military honours.	
	10/11/17		Left R.&D. CAMP & marched to WINNEZEELE arriving there about 12. 30 pm.	1 B Squadron R.N.R. Central R.N.R.

Army Form C. 2118.

WAR DIARY
or
INTELLIGENCE SUMMARY.
(Erase heading not required.)

Instructions regarding War Diaries and Intelligence Summaries are contained in F. S. Regs., Part II. and the Staff Manual respectively. Title pages will be prepared in manuscript.

Place	Date	Hour	Summary of Events and Information	Remarks and references to Appendices
	11/11/17		Left WINNEZEELE for BROXEELE, arriving there about 1.30pm.	HQ
	12/11/17		At BROXEELE. General cleaning up & reorganization.	HQ
	13/11/17		Commenced training. 4 Offrs & 177 Oth reinforcements.	HQ
	14/11/17 to 27/11/17	}	Training. Reinforcements 2 offrs 63 ORs.	HQ
	28/11/17		Left BROXEELE for NOUVEAU MONDE, arriving about 2.0pm (F.2.S.C sheet 27)	HQ
	29/11/17		Moved from NOUVEAU MONDE to ROAD CAMP (F.2.5.C sheet 27). Arrived there about 11.30 am.	HQ
	30/11/17		General cleaning up and inspection.	HQ

for Rowark, RMR
Wilson

Copy No.......

DRAKE BATTALION. ORDER NO. 2/11/17.

1. **INFORMATION** TOURNANT FARM is probably occupied by a small body of the enemy and M.Gs. Enemy has been seen in shell holes between TOURNANT FARM and SOURCE FARM.

2. **INTENTION.** TOURNANT FARM will be captured and consolidated by "B" Coy. on night of 3rd November.

3. **Instructions.**

   (a) Attack will be carried out by 5 large sections: 2 Rifle Sections of 1 N.C.O. and 15 O.Rs, 2 Bombing Sections of 1 N.C.O. and 10 men and 1 Rifle Grenade Section of 1 N.C.O. and 10 men. A reserve will be kept at SOURCE FARM of 2 Rifle Sections and 4 Lewis Guns. 2 Lewis Guns will act as covering guns, and sweep the ground between the enemy post at V.28.d.99.99. and the trees at V.28.b.70.40. These 2 points are well defined.

   (b) The attack will take place from SOURCE FARM without artillery barrage.

   (c) Company boundaries:-From V.28.d.5.7. to V.28.b.05.25 Western Boundary.
   From V.28.d.85.95. to V.28.b.40.40. Eastern boundary.

   (d) The attack will take place one hour after the troops are in position.

   (e) Communication will be established by runners to the Right Coy. H.Q. of Battalion holding Right Sub-sector (Hood Battalion).
   4 Pigeons will be taken by Coy. H.Qs. and released at dawn on morning of 4th. These pigeons will be drawn at ALBATROSS FARM on the way to the line.

   (f) Careful reconnaissance is to be carried out. O.C. "B" Coy. will stay the night of 31st at SOURCE FARM and S/Lieuts. Fegan and Southwood the nights of 1st and 2nd. respectively.

   (g) Consolidation will take place immediately after TOURNANT FARM is captured, posts pushed out, and location maps are to be sent back at frequent intervals. As much information as possible is to be sent back, and location maps must be accurate. The 2 reserve Lewis Guns will be sent forward for consolidation.

   (h) **DRESS** Haversacks on back, 24 hours rations, iron rations, water bottles full, 5 sand bags per man — carried under flap of haversack, green Flare, 1 Very Light per man. Every 2nd man a shovel, and every other man will have his rifle covered.
   Overcoats or waterproof sheets will not be carried. 1 Grenade, No. 5 per man, rifle grenade sections will carry 6 No. 20 grenades per man, 24 Lewis Gun Magazines per gun. (This supply of Lewis Gun Magazines will be left at SOURCE FARM, and sent forward to consolidating guns as required). 4 sets of S.O.S. Rockets will be carried.

   (i) A dump of 6 boxes of S.A.A. and 5 boxes of No. 5 grenades will be made at SOURCE FARM before the attack.

   (j) No stragglers will be tolerated.

   (k) There is no command - "RETIRE".

Signed W Sterndale Bennett
Commander R.N.V.R.
Commndg. Drake Battn.

WAR DIARY
or
INTELLIGENCE SUMMARY.

Army Form C. 2118.

Duke Bn
Nov 18

Place	Date	Hour	Summary of Events and Information	Remarks and references to Appendices
	1.12.17		Training at ROAD CAMP. JMJ	
	2.12.17		Left training by Coys. JMJ	
	3.12.17		Standing by to move into forward area night of 5/6. Coys practising move routes in bns in camp.	
	4.12.17		Light training by Coys. JMJ	
	5.12.17		" " "	
	6.12.17			
	7.12.17		and cleaning and packing gear before moving next day.	
	8.12.17			
	9.12.17		Leave ROAD CAMP 1.15 p.m. by road to near BAPAUME. JMJ	
	10.12.17		Near BAPAUME midday. Left at 2 p.m. for YTRICOURT where Bn. entrained for BAPAUME. Camp arrived. Bn. in huts & tents.	
	11.12.17		Training (physical, and under supervision of Specialists as per Training Programme. JMJ	
			Training (physical) and under supervision of Specialists. Lecture (by half coys) JMJ	
	12.12.17		by M.O. and Signal Officer. Orders to move afternoon of 13th to YTRICOURT. JMJ	
			Arrived YTRICOURT where Bn. encamped. JMJ	
	13.12.17		Battalion moved to METZ-EN-COUTURE. JMJ	
	14.12.17		Into Brigade Support Line at COUILLET WOOD. JMJ	
	15.12.17		Companies reconnoitring their own trenches, and commencing new line of defence. JMJ	
	16.12.17		Companies carrying out programme of work in defence system. Battalion and commencing recce work on HIGHLAND RIDGE. JMJ	
	17.12.17		Work continues as per programme. Battn. instructed also to position on night JMJ	
	18.12.17		of work as on previous days. New line continued, and one other BUSH TRENCH connecting South Spur to front line. JMJ	Marbecock Longueuel

WAR DIARY or INTELLIGENCE SUMMARY

Army Form C. 2118.

Place	Date	Hour	Summary of Events and Information	Remarks and references to Appendices
RIGHT BRIGADE	19.12.17		Move into sub sector left of LA VACQUERIE. Repairing trenches and dugouts. German Artillery and Trench Mortars very quiet all day long. Some Planes hovering over our lines all day long R.9.a. Quiet except for occasional rifle fire.	A.W.
	20.12.17		Int. very quiet. Inactivity. Two light M.Gs in area of TANK at CORNER. SUPPORT Occasional shot bursts of MG fire on our ravages in the evening "B" Coy horseted trench leading to through access to trenches in right of Coy frontage.	A.W.
	21.12.17		Enemy artillery very quiet with only a light promiscuous shelling around ARGYLLE TRENCH. Our own Artillery (field guns and Heavies) kept up a slow constant fire on enemy's line particularly in front of LA VACQUERIE and at CORNER WORK Whilst our own Trench Mortars were quite enemy fire over a few flying planes moved TANK. Our Airmen very active finding good targets – Boche moving about in the open in small numbers. Movement noticed in LA VACQUERIE and at CORNER WORK. There was no aerial activity throughout the day. At 11.15pm or 9.0 some gave two blasts of about 2 seconds duration each. Sound seems from Bn. H.Q. Exact position not ascertained. "B" Coy occupied trench about R.15.6.50.75 – R.15.8.10.45.	A.W.
	22.12.17		Enemy artillery quiet active. Shelling trenches and supports with 4.2s also ruby & stad. Railway head and Ravine R.8.c 9.0 to intermittent bursts 5.9s and 4.2s Shelling of B Coys HQ Corner Avenue. Posts established later in night. Enemy M.Gs very active. Our m.gs fixing on enemy working parties night in ruchele etc.	A.W.

WAR DIARY
or
INTELLIGENCE SUMMARY.

Army Form C. 2118.

Place	Date	Hour	Summary of Events and Information	Remarks and references to Appendices
	23.12.17		Enemy Aty. Promiscuous shelling of our forward and rear areas. Sniped and L.G. M.G. fire after rounds on enemy trench 500 yds N. of CORNER WORK. "B" Coy sent out reconnoitering patrol which sniped trench on advance of front posts successfully established the night before. Trench was unoccupied. Listening and M.G. posts were sent out and commined digging and wiring our new forward position. At 9.45 pm our artillery opened heavy fire (Field Guns and Trench Mortars) on enemy's trenches working and wiring party (250 strong). They were dispersed and did not return to their task. Enemy put down light barrage at 5.40 am & 11.20 on supports and reserves. No damage was done. Flanking fire from M.G.'s was brought to bear on enemy gun emplacements. Later our wire and trenches were exchanged between patrols. At 1.30 am enemy arty. died down. Total casualties during tour 1 killed & 4 wounded.	JMJ.
	24.12.17		Leave for MONS.	JMJ.
	25.12.17		Xmas Day. Early morning Remainder of day cleared to cleaning up and reorganising	JMJ.
	26.12.17		Inspection of equipment, clothing, etc.	JMJ.
	27.12.17		Inspection by Coy. B. C.O. of clothing equipment and daily inspection of all billets.	JMJ.
	28.12.17		Cleaning up billets before moving into front line nightfall 28/29 12.17. Enemy arty. fired very considerable damage before they went into action	JMJ.
			Relieved NELSON Bn. who went into support	JMJ.

WAR DIARY or INTELLIGENCE SUMMARY

Army Form C. 2118.

Place	Date	Hour	Summary of Events and Information	Remarks and references to Appendices
	29.12.17		B.H.Q. moved from RAVINE to WOOD AVENUE. Enemy artillery fairly active. Trench mortars playing on part of Bn. left subsector.	
	30.12.17		At 6.30 a.m. enemy laid down a heavy barrage of 77's, 5.9's & T.Ms with trench mortars and rifle grenades. At 6.45 a.m. the Boche advanced in large numbers from his newly dug trenches. Enemy were driven off everywhere except at CORNER AVENUE and northern part of CORNER SUPPORT, both entered C of No 2 TRENCH (B Coy) over where soi antiaircraft Lieut Blay's and platoon. Later in the day with the valuable assistance of the Nelson Bn. who counter-attacked over the open and from the right flank, we succeeded in driving out the enemy and establishing ourselves in our old front line. they have been preparing, moving, & everywhere kept up continued shelling of our positions. Enemy artillery heavy attack at 6 a.m. lasted till 4.15. 5 Bn. 2nd enemy attack opened silently at 9.30 a.m. in chaemy's turn. Many direct hits all day long, but slackening ofterce, were not noticeable.	
	31.12.17			

WAR DIARY
OR
INTELLIGENCE SUMMARY.

Place	Date	Hour	Summary of Events and Information	Remarks and references to Appendices
	1.1	8	Four lines outposts and companies in reserve. Artillery - Enemy not shelling the overlay. Trench mortars and Stokes barrage not interfering with our reserve. Quietened enemy guns firing. Relief by Nelson Bn.	Estimated Casualties 11 offrs + 255 OR's. Moved to Highland Ridge.

WAR DIARY or INTELLIGENCE SUMMARY

Army Form C. 2118.

Drake Bn.

Place	Date	Hour	Summary of Events and Information	Remarks and references to Appendices
In the field	1/1/18		Relieved by NELSON Bn. on front line at K.5 Highland Ridge. Bn. Battalion resting, cleaning up etc. 1 Coy. 5 Baths at H.Q. 1 Casualties.	
	2/1/18		Kept at 11 hours notice.	
	3/1/18		Bn. moved to NAVAL Trench, relieved HQ Coy. of Hood Bn., 1 Coy. Digging next Reserve line on ridge of NAVAL Trench. 2 platoons on fatigue digging & dugout next Cemetery at P.7.d. S.2. HQ Bn. Coy arrived at 11.30pm.	
	4th		Batty moved to the front line. NELSON Bn. Relieved at 11.30pm. Casualties Nil. Hurt.	
	5th		Comparison in front line. Enemy Artillery and trench mortars active. Front Line thought the day. Our artillery retaliated. Casualties 1 O.R. wounded.	
	6th		Quiet through the night. Heavy enemy trench mortars and intense Trench Mortar system. Hurt. Situation unchanged Artillery intermittent on both sides. French Mortars occasionally active.	
	7th	4.30pm	Left Coy (D.Coy) moved back into Support (NAVAL TR). Their front line Bn. HQ. and Headquarters moved from WOOD AVENUE (R.8) and re-established in RAVINE (R.14.d.99). Hood Bn. extended to R.9.c.23. Relief finish. Casualties 1 O.R. wounded. Hurt.	
	7th		2 Coys in Front Line 1 Coy in Support. Intermittent shelling on left side attack. Enemy Trench mortar batteries active. Casualties 1 O.R. killed.	
	8th		Situation unchanged. Inspection of Trenches and munitions carried out by Divisional General and Staff. French Mortars occasionally active.	
	9th	4.30pm	Bn. relieved by NELSON Bn. On wheeled transport. Billets at METZ.	
METZ	9th	1 am	Bn. arrived at METZ. Remainder of day devoted to rest and cleaning of equipment etc. Hurt.	

WAR DIARY
or
INTELLIGENCE SUMMARY
(Erase heading not required)

Army Form C. 2118.

DRAKE BATTN.

Place	Date	Hour	Summary of Events and Information	Remarks and references to Appendices
METZ	10th		Battn. at METZ. Whole of day devoted to baths, inspection of men, clothing & equipment. Battn. inspected by Medical officer. H.u.K.	
"	11th		Battn. at METZ. Inspection of men in Battle order, replacement of equipment. H.u.K.	
"	12th		Battn. at METZ. Company inspections. Cleaning up billets. Recreational training of platoons.	
"	13th		Working party supplied of 1 senior officer, 3 junior officers, 15 N.C.O. 200 o.r's for work on METZ defences. Bus shuttle dogfight in and around METZ during the afternoon. H.u.K. Company inspections, cleaning of billet areas, training of specialists. H.u.K.	
"	14th		Working party & supplied for METZ defences as detailed for 13th. H.u.K. Company inspections and specialist training. I.S.O.R. reinforcements joined Battn. H.u.K.	
"	15th			
"	16th		Parades cancelled. Wet weather. Advance parties proceed to the line. H.u.K.	
"	17th		Battalion proceeds to line relieving 1st Royal Fusiliers T/f Ahite Rifle in right sub sector of Left Divisional Front. 074 Coy holding Front line but posts. B & C Coys in support in NAVAL TRENCH. Very quiet during relief which was complete by 9.30 p.m. Heavy day notched condition, owing to being used but in enemy rockets.	
"	18th		Fairly quiet in forward areas. Heavy enemy shelling around CHARING CROSS and BEAUCAMP.	
"	19th		Intermittent shelling during day. Relieved by "Hood" Battalion to H.S. M.T.R. RIDGE. Quiet during relief which was complete by about 12.00 a.m.	
"	20th			

Army Form C. 2118.

WAR DIARY
or
INTELLIGENCE SUMMARY.
(Erase heading not required.)

Instructions regarding War Diaries and Intelligence Summaries are contained in F. S. Regs., Part II. and the Staff Manual respectively. Title pages will be prepared in manuscript.

Place	Date	Hour	Summary of Events and Information	Remarks and references to Appendices
	1917/21		Battalion in support on HIGHLAND RIDGE. Quiet.	WJB
	22nd		Relieved by 14th Battalion Royal Fusiliers, 2nd Division and moved to billets in METZ. Relief complete by 9.30pm. the evening of 22nd. Bttn during relief. WJB	
	23rd		Moved from METZ to BORASTRE Area by light railway. Relieved 22nd Bn Royal Fusiliers in TALAVERA Camp, arriving there about 8.10pm. WJB	
	24th		Cleaning up + reorganisation contd. WJB	
	25th		Training contd.	
	26th			
	27th		Inspection + Church parade. Rev.	
	28/31		Training contd.	

No previous entry contd.

Army Form C. 2118.

Drake Bn

WAR DIARY
or
INTELLIGENCE SUMMARY.
(Erase heading not required.)

Instructions regarding War Diaries and Intelligence Summaries are contained in F.S. Regs., Part II. and the Staff Manual respectively. Title pages will be prepared in manuscript.

Vol 20

Place	Date	Hour	Summary of Events and Information	Remarks and references to Appendices
	1/2/18		Training	
	2nd Feb		Training. Afternoon and evening devoted entirely to Sports and Coy. Concerts.	
	3rd "		Battalion on work of defence at NEZ. Communion service at 8.30am	
	4th "		Training.	
	5th "		Training as per programme.	
	6th "		" " " "	
	7th "		" " " "	
	8th "		" " " "	
	9th "		" " " "	
	10th "		Bn. inspection 9/15 am. Church parade 9.30am. Communion service 8.30am.	
	11th "		Training as per programme	
	12th "		" " " "	
	13th "		Reconnoitring only proceeds to line	
	14th "		Battalion moves into line CENTRE TR. (S.E. of MARCOING) - LA VACQUERIE Parts of 57c N2	
	15th "		S.E. and 57£ N.W. S.W. - L34 to 50.25 - A4 to 70.85. Relieved 9th Bn. Cheshire Regt. Relief completed	HFS Pocus W [signature] Lt Col Comdg

Army Form C. 2118.

WAR DIARY
or
INTELLIGENCE SUMMARY.

(Erase heading not required.)

Instructions regarding War Diaries and Intelligence Summaries are contained in F. S. Regs., Part II. and the Staff Manual respectively. Title pages will be prepared in manuscript.

Place	Date	Hour	Summary of Events and Information	Remarks and references to Appendices
	15.2.18		ENEMY'S ARTILLERY. Fairly active whilst relief was in progress. Salvos of 4.2" and 77mm were directed on road leading through R30 Central.	
			ENEMY'S M.G.'s. Fitful bursts of traversing fire directed for Highland Ridge.	
			HOSTILE MOVEMENT: Party of about 40 men at G7d 10.25. Fired on by m.g. fire	
	16.2.18		OPERATIONS: At 5.25 am enemy put down a 7 m. and light shell bombardment on sunken Road at L34 Central and entrenches in rear. Infantry closely followed barrage. A German raiding party of from 50 to 60 men who came from the direction of L34 d 15.35 and entered the garrison exits the N.G.O. trench were moving. Two wounded, one dead German lay in the front of the L.G. post and his cap (R.O.I.R. 7 stated that trick) lay near and shortly there were sent to Bde. early this morning	
			OUR ARTILLERY. Carrying out trench shots on enemy line. Visibility excellent	
	17.2.18		Artillero Inactive whole of day. Quite normal. Infantry quiet	
	18.2.18		With exception of occasional shelling of Itolyn", and main line noth LR0 and a few rounds fired from hostile level mortar light on night of Icondrole	

A7093. Wt. W12839/M1292. 750,000. 1/17. D. D. & L., Ltd. Forms/C2118/11.

Army Form C. 2118.

WAR DIARY
or
INTELLIGENCE SUMMARY.
(Erase heading not required.)

Instructions regarding War Diaries and Intelligence Summaries are contained in F. S. Regs., Part II. and the Staff Manual respectively. Title pages will be prepared in manuscript.

Place	Date	Hour	Summary of Events and Information	Remarks and references to Appendices
	18.2.18		There is nothing particular to note. During the afternoon three trams were seen moving on the MARCOING-MAGNIERES narrow-gauge railway. These trams were seen moving at their usual and were pulling on the average six to ten covered trucks. There seems to be a steady movement north of MARCOING COPSE thro' the light railway engines come to rest. There was also much movement on the road LYNE from MARCOING at about N. of MARCOING COPSE light railway siding. Two motor wagons and three GS wagons were noted on this road for over an hour and various others. (Presumably ration parties) were seen to come to a point on this road and to ascend to a point on this road is beyond field gun range being about 6000 yds from OP at BruZO, unbroken Alley. Relieved by ANSON BN. A great number of Gondolellas were put into RAILWAY VALLEY just north of WOOD AVENUE while the relief was in progress, the relief was carried out in town. — Battalion moves down to TRESCAULT where it entrained and after detraining afoot over VALLULET CAMP, LECHELLE-YPRES Road. Remainder of day devoted mainly to cleaning up of clothes and equipment.
	20.2.18		Light training as per programme. Learn from instructors in afternoon Battalion moves into BERTINCOURT taking over hutts of 1/5 R London Regt.	
	21st "			
	22nd "		Battalion entrains for TRESCAULT and relieves 23rd London Regt. in RIBECOURT — A Base D Coys in forward Rouine RIBECOURT C Coy. in close support to MONTIE BN.	HQ Ribcourt

WAR DIARY
or
INTELLIGENCE SUMMARY

Army Form C. 2118.

Place	Date	Hour	Summary of Events and Information	Remarks and references to Appendices
RIBECOURT.	23rd		Battn. in TAISET TRENCH L.20 a and and L.26 a and b. Brigade Support.	
"	24th		Fld. Battn. newly built, with occasional shelling of valley south of Ribecourt.	
"	25th		Lieut. Johnson's trench batt.	
"	26th		A Coy. relieved C Coy. in clear support to Hauorts battn. which relieved the H.O.O.T's tonight. B Coy. working in KAISER TR. B Coy. working into the line in afternoon on PREMY. AVE. C Coy. working on the right at night.	
"	27th		Heavy barrage opened out during the early morning by our guns. One ENEMY AIROPLANE brought down at L.2.B.B.15.95 at 11.15 am.	
"	29th		Nothing to report.	

NOTE:— During the past stay in RIBECOURT good opportunity has been afforded for all men having a good bath in the village. The Regimental canteen was also in full swing.

H.G. Peacock
Col. R.W.F.

189th Brigade.
63rd Division.

"D R A K E" BATTALION

M A R C H   1 9 1 8

WAR DIARY
or
INTELLIGENCE SUMMARY.

Place	Date	Hour	Summary of Events and Information	Remarks and references to Appendices
In the field	Mar 1st		In RIBECOURT. Working parties on Front Line System. M.	
	2		Relieved HOOD Battalion in RIBECOURT Centre Sub sector of Divisional Front. In front line. Quiet. P.M.	
	3/5		In Front Line. Quiet.	
	6		Relieved by HAWKE Battalion, & moved to WESTWOOD CAMP (C & D Coys) & TRESCAULT (HQ, A & B Coys) in Divl Reserve. Relief complete 12.30 a.m. M?	
	7		Cleaning up & refitting of troops. M?	
	8/10		Training. On 9th Summer time came into force at 11. on 8th M?	
	11.		Training.	
	12.		Heavy enemy gas bombardment took place, all along TRESCAULT VALLEY, which continued for five hours. M? A & B Coys were gassed. 2 Offrs & 392 ORs gassed. Command in D.M.N. Beak, M.C. took command of Battalion. M?	
	13.		Carried on training with C & D Coys. M? 1 Officer (Lieut. M. PERSON) & 219 ORs from 7th Batt. M? Battn. Reinforcements joined for duty.	

WAR DIARY
or
INTELLIGENCE SUMMARY.
(Erase heading not required.)

Army Form C. 2118.

Place	Date	Hour	Summary of Events and Information	Remarks and references to Appendices
In the Field	15.		Relieved HOOD Bn in front line system at RIBECOURT. Relief complete by 10.30 pm.	Relief 11 pm
	16/17		In front line. Quiet.	
	18/19.		Right Coy sector "staged" by Heavy TM's. Light TM's. Relieved on night of 19th by HAWKE Bn. Relief complete by 11.00 pm. Battalion moved into support in MINE TRENCH, UNSEEN SUPPORT & UNSEEN TRENCH. Battn HQ in UNSEEN TRENCH.	11 pm
	20		In support. Quiet.	
	21.		Beginning of GERMAN Offensive. Heavy gas bombardment of UNSEEN TRENCH system for five hours with "mustard gas". RIBECOURT with "phosgene gas" from 6.30 am onwards till midday. Heavy barrage of all calibre shells was maintained on the support system RIBECOURT. By 11.00 a.m. the enemy was in possession of 20 right posts of front line. Battalion relieved HAWKE Battn in BEET TRENCH, part of NIGGER & KAISER TRENCH.	

WAR DIARY
or
INTELLIGENCE SUMMARY.

Army Form C. 2118.

Place	Date	Hour	Summary of Events and Information	Remarks and references to Appendices
Little	21.		Relief completed by 9.00 pm. Support coys commenced to withdraw at 11.00 pm.	
Feb	22.		By 3.00 am the Battn. had successfully withdrawn to the UNSEEN Trench System. Heavy bombardment of RIBECOURT till 10.00 am when German scouts were seen coming through the village towards the system. At 10.00 pm we commenced our withdrawal to NEUVILLE. Rearguard left UNSEEN Trenty system at 12.30 am 23rd March.	
	23.		At 2.30 am we evacuated the 1b British front line (HERMIES TRESAULT Line) & proceeded via TRESCAULT Flank Roads through HAVRINCOURT WOOD to NEUVILLE, where we arrived at 5.00 am. Batalion moved at 12 noon in the direction of YTRES, & at 1.00 pm commenced to dig in, in front of YTRES. 190th Bde held right front, 76th Bde left front. All quiet until 4.00 pm when eight field were fired into the village. By 9.00 pm the 4th & 7th divn. had withdrawn from right of 190th Bde, leaving flank exposed. No line of ? flank was formed by swinging back	

WAR DIARY
INTELLIGENCE SUMMARY

Army Form C. 2118.

Place	Date	Hour	Summary of Events and Information	Remarks and references to Appendices
	24		190th Bde, + A + D Coys of DRAKES through R.E. DUMP, YPRES and along the BUS-HOUSE-YPRES Road. This was completed at 5. a.m. We commenced to withdraw on this day under a very barrage of H.E. shrapnel to BEAUCOURT via BORESIRE. After two hours rest, we withdrew from BEAUCOURT about 3 companys + proceeded to a position in HIGH WOOD via FIERS. Our casualties up to this time were extremely light. Lt. Commr TURRELL M.C. 'missing presumed killed.' T/Surgeon N.A.H. NICKERSON 'missing, believed prisoner of war.' No rations received on this day. A large German patrol proceeded along valley on far side of HIGH WOOD. Another with Very Lights + Machine Guns. An exceptionally quiet night was spent.	
	25		By 2. a.m. our right flank was again exposed owing to withdrawal of 17th 2 Dubn. From daybreak onwards Rifle + M/y fire was carried on. At 9. a.m. DRAKE Batt. advanced 17-17 + D.2 S.T.O. and captured three Machine Guns. One of which was turned on the retiring enemy.	

WAR DIARY
or
INTELLIGENCE SUMMARY

(Erase heading not required.)

Place	Date	Hour	Summary of Events and Information	Remarks and references to Appendices
	25.		About 10.0 a.m. orders were received to withdraw to ridge behind the village of MARTINPUICH. (COURCELETTE road). This was successfully carried out, but with heavy losses. On the COURCELETTE Road a stand was made, to cover withdrawal of the 2nd Divn. on the left of our Divl. frontage we withdrew in a regular fashion to THIEPVAL. 189th Inf Bde guarded the ridge across the ANCRE on the north side of HAMEL. No rations were got up on this day. J.M.	
	26.		At 3.0 a.m. we withdrew across the ANCRE & manned the old trenches N. of railway. This was completed by 5.0 a.m. only fine became rather intense about 11.0 a.m. from our left flank. Our heavy artillery (6"?) started to drop short on railway about 3.00 p.m. & continued like that for a period of two hours, causing severe casualties until wire provided. Relieved by 6th Batln. the QUEENS. at 10.00 p.m. when we proceed to ENGEL BELMER via MESNIL. J.M.	

WAR DIARY
or
INTELLIGENCE SUMMARY

(Erase heading not required.)

Place	Date	Hour	Summary of Events and Information	Remarks and references to Appendices
	27.		At 11.30 a.m. troops received hot food then dug in in front of ENGELBELMER, placing strong piquets on the roads approaching the village. At 9.0 a.m. we surrendered to billets.	
	28/ 29.		Refitting of troops in ENGELBELMER. Moves to HAILLY-MAILLET taken one hour stay, returned to former billets in ENGELBELMER.	
	30.		Batt. moves to HEDAUVILLE at 9.15 a.m. Engelbelmer was shelled as we left: casualties 2 o/ro killed, 12 o.r. wounded.	
	31.		Carry on training	

Total Casualties for Operations 27/31 inclusive

16 officers + 10 o.r. O.R.

W.N.W. Beak R.N.V.R.
Comdr.
Comdr DRAKE BN

189th Brigade.
63rd Divison

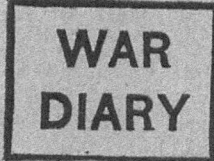

DRAKE BATTALION

APRIL 1 9 1 8

1. Drake Battn.

WAR DIARY or INTELLIGENCE SUMMARY for April 1918.

Place	Date	Hour	Summary of Events and Information	Remarks and references to Appendices
In the field	July 1st		HEDAUVILLE. Training by Companies	
	2nd		Batn marched to HERRISART via FORCEVILLE, ACHEUX, LEALVILLERS and TOUTENCOURT.	
	3rd		Batn: marched to FORCEVILLE, via TOUTENCOURT, HARPONVILLE and VARENNES.	
	4,5 + 6th		FORCEVILLE. Training by Companies.	
	7,8		Batn relieved 1/4th Royal Fusiliers in ENGLEBELMER in Support.	
	8.		Slight gas shelling.	
	9,10,11th		Working parties.	
	11?		Batn: relieved Hawke Bn in front line, to the front and left of MESNIL.	
	12,13,14th		FRONT LINE. Relieved by East Yorks Regt 17th Div, relief being complete by 11.0 p.m.	
	15th		Batn: arrived in FORCEVILLE from line whence from reserve by encampture two 17th Div.	
	16th		Batn: proceeded to TOUTENCOURT via ACHEUX + LEALVILLERS. Reorganization of Companies.	
	17,18,19,20,22		Batn: Carried on training and Working parties.	
	23rd			

WAR DIARY
or
INTELLIGENCE SUMMARY. for April 1918.

Place	Date	Hour	Summary of Events and Information	Remarks and references to Appendices
Authville	24th		Battn moved to BOIS-CREPPEL and carried on usual training.	
	25.		Battn Carried on usual training.	
	26,27,28			
	29.		Battn moved with Brigade on manoeuvres to HEDAUVILLE-FORCEVILLE	
	30		line, digging in on left of FORCEVILLE	

CASUALTIES.

	Killed	Wounded
Officers.	—	3
ORs.	1	14

J Clarke Lt. RNVR Adjutant
for Comdr RNVR
Commanding O.C. A.G.B.
Bn.

Army Form C. 2118.

"DRAKE BATT" WAR DIARY MAY 1918
INTELLIGENCE SUMMARY.
(Erase heading not required.)

Instructions regarding War Diaries and Intelligence Summaries are contained in F. S. Regs., Part II. and the Staff Manual respectively. Title pages will be prepared in manuscript.

WO 93

Place	Date	Hour	Summary of Events and Information	Remarks and references to Appendices
Toutencourt	1st to 7th		Company and Battalion training - Working Party of 260 men every other day to the Brown Line East of FORCEVILLE	✓
MESNIL	Night 8/9		Relieved 10th Notts + Derby Regt in MESNIL A + D in front line B + C in Support line - Relief complete by 12.10 am	✓
	10th to 14th		Tunnel Warfare - improvement of trenches - Wiring of Outposts - Shelling of Enemy transport on HAMEL - BEAUCOURT Road.	✓
FORCEVILLE	14/15		Relieved by HAWKE Battalion - Relief complete 1.20 am. Moved to Sunken Road South of FORCEVILLE + became Reserve Batt B Coy to Bank E of Englebelmer	✓
	16th to 19th		Specialist training - Remainder of Batt= Working Party	✓
Englebelmer	20th		Relieved HOOD BATTALION in BANKS EAST of ENGLEBELMER (Support) to D Coy relieved 1 Company (HOOD BATT") in Bank at MESNIL - attached to Front line Batt" (HOOD BATT") for Work and operations.	✓
	21st to 23rd		Night Working parties to Front line system	✓
	24th		D Coy moved up + occupied front line A Coy took over DCys line	✓
MESNIL	25th		while HOOD RAID was in operation Battalion relieved HOOD Batt" in front line at MESNIL Relief complete 12.55 am.	✓

Army Form C. 2118.

WAR DIARY
or
INTELLIGENCE SUMMARY.

for May Cont?

(Erase heading not required.)

Instructions regarding War Diaries and Intelligence Summaries are contained in F.S. Regs., Part II. and the Staff Manual respectively. Title pages will be prepared in manuscript.

Place	Date	Hour	Summary of Events and Information	Remarks and references to Appendices
MESNIL	26th	4pm	Enemy heavily bombarded our line with Trench Mortars — Artillery mainly on the Main Line of Resistance (Up to n Trench) S.O.S sent up by Right Brigade but no Infantry action followed.	※
	27th		BARN TRENCH shelled by 5.9's during the afternoon	※
	28th 30th		Slight shelling by Artillery + Trench Mortars but very much quieter than preceding days.	※
	31/5		Relieved by HAWKE BATT.n - Relief coy. at 12.15 am Batt. moved to Forceville in reserve. Heavy bombardment and attack by divisions on our right. Canal line.	※
			Killed Officers — Wounded 1 — 3	Other Ranks Field Killed Wounded 15 - 54

O.W.B. Beak Commanding R.N.V.R.
Commanding DRAKE BATTn

DRAKE BATT" WAR DIARY for June 1918

Army Form C. 2118.

Instructions regarding War Diaries and Intelligence Summaries are contained in F. S. Regs., Part II. and the Staff Manual respectively. Title pages will be prepared in manuscript.

INTELLIGENCE SUMMARY.
(Erase heading not required.)

Place	Date	Hour	Summary of Events and Information	Remarks and references to Appendices
FORCEVILLE	1-6-18 to 3-6-18		Reserve Battⁿ in RANKS 2 FORCEVILLE. Carried on Platoon and Specialist Training	
PUISEMPRE	4-6-18		Relieved by 17th R.W.F. at 4pm & marched to Rupempre. Took over from 13th R.W.F. Much Discipline very good. Battⁿ at —	
	5th to 7th		Baths by 1pm	
	8th		Cleaning up & resting	
	9th		Platoon & Specialist Training	
			Church Parade & presentation of medals to 2 prisoners I knot	
	10th to 15th		Monday see Friday by B.O.C 189 Inf Brigade	
	16th		Platoon & Specialist Training	
	17th &		Church Parade	
	19th		Company Training on attack, advance & Rear Guards	
	20th		Battalion Show	
	21st		Company Training	
	22nd		Company Training	
Auchonvillers	23rd		Left Rubempre at 9am & marched to Acheux Wood arriving 11am. Rested until 9pm & then relieved 16th Royal Irish Reg^t in support S. of Auchonvillers - Relief complete 12.40am. Front & Rear areas very quiet - No casualties	

Army Form C. 2118.

DRAKE Bn WAR DIARY for June Cont'd
or
INTELLIGENCE SUMMARY.
(Erase heading not required.)

Place	Date	Hour	Summary of Events and Information	Remarks and references to Appendices
MUCRONVILLERS	24th to 29th		Working parties from Support Batt'n to Front line running in front of Locality A9 also parties under R.E. making deep dugouts in mountain front of the line. During tour quiet the whole time. One man wounded.	DO216
	29th/30th	1.20 a.m.	Relieved Hood Bn in advanced forward zone relief complete by 1.20 a.m. Back areas heavily shelled	Appx

D. Galloway
Lieut. Colonel
Officer Commanding
Drake Battalion

WAR DIARY DRAKE BATTⁿ
INTELLIGENCE SUMMARY
July 1918

Army Form C. 2118.

Place	Date	Hour	Summary of Events and Information	Remarks and references to Appendices
MAILLY RIGHT SECTOR	1st to 5th		Holding front line on new system of locality and strong points of all own & camp closely wired round. A Company on left & in centre. B on right with Battⁿ. B Company in support. Received warning that the Battⁿ must show volentification either by a Battle Patrol or Raid. Patrols managed to the ordinary extent & found to be occupied by Scott Battalion a crater found at Bucket Buckden Road a9 Q17 Central, otherwise no enemy encountered. Road decided upon a D. Coy detail to proceed with execution scheme. Relieved by HAWKE BATTⁿ — took over Battⁿ Battⁿ Quarters in Reserve in the Purple system EAST of MAILLY MAILLET	
	Night 5/6			
	6th to 11th		Two Companies working parties said night. B Coy line commenced training for a small model of enemy line to be raided East man constructed in late particular part — then practiced as a will particular part company detail as the sum itself	

WAR DIARY
or
INTELLIGENCE SUMMARY.

Army Form C. 2118.

Place	Date	Hour	Summary of Events and Information	Remarks and references to Appendices
AUCHON-VILLERS	Night 11/12		Relieved HOOD Battalion in support on MAILLY–RIGHT 25TH SOUTH of AUCHONVILLERS. Large raid by RWF on the night under cover of what we continued noise cutting on crater at 9.17 central.	
	12/13		Raid was carried out. ZERO at Midnight. Party consisted of 2nd Lieut Buckler & Bolt and 52 O.Rs. Lieut Robertson I/C. D.Cy was Commander of raid. Position raided was approximately 1000 yards N of HAMEL. The men were in excellent spirits & confident of success. They were ready in their lying out position by 11.45 p.m. & on the stroke of midnight! moved to1 formed at ZERO plus 4 charged the crater & enemy line. The raid was a great success. Casualties 4 wounded and 1 missing - Captured - 23 m.m. 2 M.G. 1 heavy & a light 1 L.M.G. brought back - Revolver and equipment.	

WAR DIARY
or
INTELLIGENCE SUMMARY

Army Form C. 2118.

Place	Date	Hour	Summary of Events and Information	Remarks and references to Appendices
ACHONVILLERS	16th 17th		In support to 11th Battalion during enemy front line + shell not retaliate afterwards.	
	Night 17th/18th		Relieved Hood Battalion in front line. Enemy very quiet. Relief complete 10.40 p.m. 17th.	
	18th to 25th		Front line Battalion. Nil to record. Patrols endeavoured to get up to S.W. side of HAMEL trench system to find how enemy had been relieved during the night 23/24 in thin machine gun + rifle were much more than	
	Night 25/26		Relieved by 15th Durham Light Infantry (21st Division) Relief complete 12.5 a.m.	
	26th		Battalion marched back to ACHEUX where Battalion rested during the night & then marched to Puchvillers at 7 am morning of 27th	
	28th 29th		Clearing up + Church parade. Bn to MARIEUX by lorry + march to LOUVENCOURT	
	30th 31		Drove the enemy at ? & by ? ? + 4 p.m. + sparkle + Reg. Commenced platoon + training. Ohl Beak	

Army Form W.3091.

Cover for Documents.

REPORT ON RAID CARRIED OUT BY "D R A K E" BATTALION on 12th/13th JULY 1918.

Nature of Enclosures.

CONTENTS.

SECTION I ... General Preparations for Raid.
SECTION II ... Plan.
SECTION III ... Execution.
SECTION IV ... Notes & Lessons.

APPENDICES.

APPENDIX 'A' ... 63rd (RN) DIVISIONAL ORDER.
APPENDIX 'B' ... 189th Infantry Brigade Order.
APPENDIX 'C' ... "DRAKE" Battalion Order.
APPENDIX 'D' ... 'D' Company "DRAKE" Battalion Order.
APPENDIX 'E' ... 63rd (RN) Divisional Artillery Order.
APPENDIX 'F' ... 63rd Machine Gun Battalion Order.
APPENDIX 'G' ... V Corps H.A. Instructions. ✗
APPENDIX 'H' ... Counter Battery Instructions. ✗

MAPS.

'X' ... General Map of Operation.
'Y' ... Artillery Barrage.
'Z' ... Machine Gun Barrage.

✗ *Not enclosed*

Notes, or Letters written.

SECRET.

APPENDIX 'a'.

Copy No......

Map Ref:- Trench Map 1/10,000.
Part of 57d. S.E.

63rd (RN) DIVISION ORDER No. 247.

RAID. 1. The 189th Infantry Brigade will carry out a Raid on the night 12th/13th July 1918 with the object of -

    (a) Capturing and killing Germans - as many prisoners to be taken as possible.

    (b) Obtaining identifications and documents.

    (c) Capturing Machine Guns.

2. OBJECTIVES.

    (a) 1st Objective. Enemy's Trench, "LUSTRE SUPPORT" from Q.17.d.20.77. to Q.17.central.

    (b) 2nd Objective. To exploit the success of (a) by clearing up "LOUNGE TRENCH" from Q.17.d.42.77. to Q.17.b.12.18.

3. Strength of Raiding Party. One Officer as O/C., Raid with 2 Officers and 52 O.R.

4. Zero Hour. (The hour at which the Artillery bombardment will open) will be fixed by the 189th Infantry Brigade and communicated to Divisional Headquarters by 10.0 am. 12th July, by whom it will be notified to all concerned.

5. Artillery Support. The C.R.A. will arrange -

    (a) To cut the necessary wire before the date of the operation. Wire on other parts of the Divisional front to be cut at the same time.

    (b) For the requisite Field and Heavy Artillery support. (A copy of the Artillery programme to be forwarded to Divisional Headquarters).

6. Machine Gun Support. The Officer Commanding 63rd Machine Gun Battalion will (in consultation with the C.R.A.) arrange for the Machine Gun support required. (A copy of the Machine Gun programme to be forwarded to Divisional Headquarters).

7. Light Signal. A rifle grenade bursting into 2 RED and 2 WHITE Lights will be fired three times in succession from our front line trench opposite the point raided, under orders to be issued by the O.C., Raid, as soon as all the raiders have returned. On this signal the Artillery and Machine Gun barrage will die down.

8. Synchronization of Watches.

    (a) A General Staff Officer from Divisional Headquarters will synchronize the watches of the undermentioned at their respective Headquarters at the following hours on the 12th July:-

        C.R.A................ 5.0. pm.
        63rd M.G.Battn..... 5.30.pm.
        189th Inf. Bde..... 5.45.pm.

    (b) The C.R.A. will arrange to synchronize the watches of the H.A., and flanking Artilleries taking part in the operation.

9.   ACKNOWLEDGE.

                                    (Sgd.) W. G. NEILSON,
                                           Lieutenant Colonel,
                                              General Staff,
8th July 1918.   63rd (RN.) Division.

Issue to Signals at :- 11.0.pm.

DISTRIBUTION:-

              Copy No. 1.   O.O.File.
                      2-3.   War Diary.
                      4-6.   A.A. & Q.M.G.
                      7.   63rd Div. Arty.
                      8.   63rd Div. Engrs.
                      9.   188th Inf. Bde.
                      10.   189th Inf. Bde.
                      11.   190th Infantry Bde.
                      12.   63rd M. G. Battn
                      13-14. V Corps.
                      15.   V Corps H.A.
                      16.   V Corps R.A.

SECRET.

63rd (Rn) Division. No.Ga.5/19.

63rd Div. Arty.
63rd Div. Engrs.
188th Inf. Bde.
189th Inf. Bde.
190th Inf. Bde.
63rd M.G.Battn.
"Q"
Vth Corps H.A.
Vth Corps R.A..

1.   Reference 63rd (RN) Division Order No. 247, paragraph 4 –

    ZERO hour will be 12.0 midnight on night 12/13th July 1918.

2.   ACKNOWLEDGE.

12th July 1918.

(sd) W.R. MEREDITH, Major,
for
Lieutenant Colonel.
General Staff.
63rd (RN) Division.

SECRET.   Copy No...9....

"DRAKE" BATTALION OPERATION ORDER NO.21.

Reference Map - sheet 57d. S.E. 1/20,000.   8th July 1918.

INTENTION. 1. "D" Coy. will carry out a raid on the night of 12/13th inst. on the Brigade front. ZERO hour to be notified later.

OBJECTIVE. 2. To raid LUSTRE SUPPORT Trench from Q.17.d.2.7. to Crater at Q.17. contral. If no prisoners are taken in this or if the Officer on the spot thinks the enemy are demoralised, to continue the attack and clear up LOUNGE Trench from Q.17.d.4.7. to Q.17.b.1.2.

OBJECT. 3. (a) To obtain identification, i.e. prisoners, documents, etc.
(b) To put as large a number as possible of the enemy out of action.
(c) To demolish dug-outs and capture arms, etc.

STRENGTH. 4. Raiding Party of 2 Officers, 2 P.Os. and 50 O.Rs, which will be organised as follows :-
"A" Party - Sub.Lieut.BOLT,1 P.O. & 25 O.Rs.
"B" Party - Sub.Lt.BRIDDON(O.C.Raiding Party),1 P.O. and 25 O.Rs.
Covering Party (Lewis Gun) - 1 N.C.O. & 6 O.Rs.

O.C. RAID. 5. Lieut. W.A. ROBERTSON.M.C., who will establish his Battle H.Q. in dugout in BEAUMONT Trench at approximately Q.17.a.6.1. by ZERO minus 1 Hour, accompanied by his Battle H.Q. Personnel, viz:- 2 Sigs,2 Runners,6 Stretcher Bearers and 3 Stretchers.

O.C. RAIDING PARTY. 6. Sub.Lieut. H.B. BRIDDON. R.N.V.R.

OFFICER i/c FORMING UP. 7. The Battalion Intelligence Officer, Sub.Lieut.S.W.G. WALKER.M.M. accompanied by 3 Runners from Battn.H.Q.

COVERING PARTY. 8. Sub.Lieut. G.HUNTER accompanied by one runner from "C" Coy.,will be responsible for placing the covering party of 1 Lewis Gun Section in position, in the old Trench at Q.17.a.75.15. He will report to Battle H.Q. that this has been done by ZERO - 10 Minutes. In addition he is responsible for the return of the covering party at the conclusion of the raid.

PRELIMINARY DISPOSITIONS. 9. At ZERO minus 2½ Hours.
The party will move off from the Support Position in the following order at 3 minutes interval:-
(a) O.C.,Raid and Battle H.Q.
(b) Sub.Lieut.HUNTER and covering party.
(c) Sub.Lieut. WALKER and 3 runners.
(d) "A" Raiding Party.
(e) "B"   do.
(f) Forward Battalion H.Q.

METHOD OF ATTACK. 10. (a) At ZERO minus 45 minutes the Raiding Party will leave the trench at Q.17.c.4.4. and will form up along the track with their right at the junction of the track & trench at Q.17.c.7.6. by ZERO minus 10 mins. under the supervision of the Battalion Intelligence Officer who will report the party in position by runner to O.C.Raid.
(b) The barrage will open at ZERO on LUSTRE SUPPORT, LOUNGE & LOCUST Trenches. It will lift off LUSTRE SUPPORT at ZERO plus 4 Minutes and off LOUNGE at ZERO plus 6 mins. When the guns lift off these trenches they will join a box barrage already formed 150 yards from the FINAL Objective (i.e.LOUNGE Trench from Q.17.d.4.7. to Q.17.b.1.2.
(c) At ZERO the Raiding Party will close up to the barrage as near as possible, at ZERO plus 4 minutes they will rush the Trench and Crater, subsequently working along LUSTRE SUPPORT and the new trench at Q.17.central to LOUNGE Trench.

WITHDRAWAL. 11. No general signal will be given from our trenches for the withdrawal. When O.C.,Raiding Party,Sub.Lt. BRIDDON thinks that the time for withdrawal has arrived he will blow a whistle. This signal will be taken up by all N.C.Os. and the Raiding Party will then withdraw

The Raiding Party will return via the old trench running west from Q.17. central to A.7. locality where they will be met by the Intelligence Officer and conducted to Batn. H.Q.

TERMINATING SIGN. 12. The return of the Raiding Party to our trenches will be signalled by three rockets (colours of which will be notified later) and fullerphone, upon which the artillery fire will cease. The Battn. Intelligence Officer will be responsible for these signals.

NATURE OF COVERING FIRE. 13. The Barrage on LUSTRE SUPPORT will consist of 18-pndrs. and five Stokes Mortars.
On LOUNGE and the new Trench of 18-pndrs, 4.3 Hows., and 3 Stokes Mortars. The standing and box barrages will consist of Heavy Artillery, using a large proportion of H.E., Trench Mortars and Machine Gun.
Covering fire from Artillery and Machine Guns will be placed on the German trenches on the opposite side of the valley in Q.17.c. & d. and Q.23.b., STATION ROAD valley, and the slopes on the north east side of it.

FORWARD BATTN. H.Q. 14. These willbe established at Q.16.b.2.6. in A.4. Locality by ZERO minus 1 hour.

SYNCHRONISATION OF WATCHES. 15. At 7.30 p.m. on 12th inst., all Officers proceeding forward will send their watches to Battn. H.Q. for adjustment to correct Brigade Time.

APPENDICES. 16. Instructions relative to Dress, etc. Equipment, Medical arrangements, signals, etc. in connection with these orders are annexed in the form of Appendices.

D. Galloway,
Lieut. Commdr. R.N.V.R.,
Commdg. DRAKE Battalion.

Copies issued to:-
Copy No. 1. C.O.
2. O.C., Raid.
3. Battn. Intelligence Officer.
4. O.C., "A" Coy.
5. O.C., "B" Coy.
6. O.C., "C" Coy.
7. 189th Infy. Brigade.
8. O.C., HAWKE Battalion.
9. War Diary.
10. File.
11. Spare.
12. "

APPENDIX No. 1.

To be read in conjunction with Operation Order No. 21.

DRESS. 1. Rifle, Bayonet and Bandolier, Steel Helmets, S.B.Rs., Field Dressings, Special Identity Discs. Every man will carry two bombs, one in each bottom tunic pocket. In addition 16 "P" bombs will be carried, which will be equally distributed, and 20 Rifle Grenades.

All Numerals, Badges, Identity Discs, Pay Books, Private Correspondence, and any other means of Identification will be packed in the Haversack, which will be stored under Guard at Coy. H.Q.

Officers - Equipment as above, but xxxxx will carry revolvers.

MEALS. 2. The Q.M. will arrange for extra rations to be issued to O.C., "D" Coy. in order that the raiding party may receive a hot meal before proceeding forward.

An extra tea, milk & sugar ration will also be issued to O.C., "D" Coy. who will detail 1 Cook and a carrying party to take up to the Right Forward Coy. Cook-House all the necessary gear (including drinking vessels) required for the preparation of tea.

Every man will receive one pint of tea before ZERO minus 45 minutes, and on return to their Coy. Area will receive a Rum ration.

APPENDIX.   No. II.

To be read in conjunction with Operation Order No. 21.

MEDICAL ARRANGEMENTS.

BEARER POST.

1. 6 Stretcher Bearers and 3 Stretchers will be established at Battle H. Qrs.

AID POSTS.

2. The Battalion Medical Officer, Medical Corporal, 6 Stretcher Bearers and 3 Stretchers will be established at Forward Battalion H. Qrs.

   m All Stretcher cases and walking cases will return via A.7 locality ETON LANE.

APPENDIX No. III.

To be read in conjunction with Operation Order No. 21.

SIGNAL ARRANGEMENTS.

Communication will be established between Battle H.Qrs. and Forward Battalion H.Qrss by Fullerphone by 6.0 p.m. on 12th Inst.

The following code will be used in sending messages to Brigade Headquarters, and signal forms will be made out ready for transmission as the times are reported to O.C., Raid.

MESSAGE.	CODE.	TIME.
Raiding Party arrived in Front Line.	"Door"	....
Raiding Party starting from Q.17.c.4.4.	"WINDOW"	....
Covering Party in position.	"ROOM"	....
Raiding Party in position.	"KITCHEN"	....
Raid started.	"TABLE"	....
Raiding Party returned.	"CHAIR"	....
Covering Party returned	"SOFA"	....

FINAL MESSAGE. - Result of Raid in Clear.

When Battle H.Qrs. are being vacated after the raid, the fullerphone will be disconnected and brought back by the Signallers to the Reserve Position.

S E C R E T.   APPENDIX "E".

63rd (RN) DIVISIONAL ARTILLERY OPERATION ORDER No. 204.

Ref. Map:- Part of　　　　　　　　　　　　　Headquarters, R.A.
Sheet 57D.S.E. 1/10,000.　　　　　　　　　　　9th July 1918.

1.　　On the night 12th/13th July 1918, the 189th Infantry Brigade will carry out a raid.

　　　　1st Objective.　Enemy's Trench "LUSTRE SUPPORT" from Q.17.d.20.77. to Q.17.central.

　　　　2nd Objective.　To exploit the success of (a) by clearing up "LOUNGE TRENCH" from Q.17.d.42.77. to Q.17.b.12.18.

2.　　The 63rd (RN) Divisional Artillery, with the assistance of flank D.A's., will cover this operation in co-ordination with machine guns.
　　　　"Silent" guns will take part.

3.　　The Corps Heavy Artillery are co-operating with a programme, the nature of which is shown on attached tracing.
　　　　Counter Battery work is arranged for.

4.　　Sufficient ammunition must be dumped beforehand so that the normal amount per gun is in the positions after these operations are over.

5.　　Brigade Commanders will please ensure that the nature and extent of hostile Artillery action in reply is recorded and reported as soon as possible to these Headquarters.

6.　　LIGHT SIGNAL.　A rifle grenade bursting into two RED and two WHITE lights will be fired three times in succession from our front line trench opposite the point raided, under orders to be issued by the O.C. Raid, as soon as all the raiders have returned.
　　　　This will be the signal for all guns to cease fire.
　　　　This light will be immediately repeated from the Brigade O.P's at Q.3.c.35.50., Q.1.d.8.8. and Q.8.d.99.20., and information that the light has been seen and repeated will be sent by telephone from these O.Ps. to Artillery Brigade H.Q.
　　　　Arrangements will be made to pass the "Cease Fire" on to the flank Brigades of neighbouring Divisions. Flank D.As. will also be informed by these H.Q.

7.　　The Artillery Arrangements are attached.

8.　　ZERO HOUR will be notified later.

9.　　Arrangements for synchronization of watches for all Artillery will be made by 63rd (RN) Divisional Artillery Signal Officer on 12th July.

10.　　No mention of this operation is to be made over the telephone.

11.　　ACKNOWLEDGE.

　　　　　　　　　　　　　　　(Sgd) H. E. YATES, Major R.F.A.,
　　　　　　　　　　　　　　　　　　　A/Brigade Major,
　　　　　　　　　　　　　　　　63rd (RN) Divisional Artillery.

DISTRIBUTION:-

SECRET.

M.G./1143.

63rd (RN) Div. M.G. Battalion.

11.7.18.

All recipients of
63rd M.G. Bn. O.O.42.

1. The O.C. Raid is sending up from different points of the front line a series of Green asteroid signal rockets, (50 small stars bursting into a cone) from ZERO plus 6 till the raiding party returns to indicate to the raiding party the position of our line.

2. The cease fire signal upon which all Machine Guns will cease fire is a grenade rocket bursting into two red and two white lights fired from the front line at Q.17.a.6.1.

3. Amend para.3, "D" Company, second task, for Q.10.b.0.9. read Q.10.b.9.0.

4. ZERO HOUR will be 12 midnight 12/13th July, 1918.

5. M.G. Companies and 38th Battalion M.G.C. to acknowledge.

(sd) E. SIMPSON Capta and Adjt.,
for O.C. 63rd (RN) Div.M.G.Battalion.

SECRET.   Copy No. 12

"D" Coy. DRAKE BATTALION OPERATION ORDER FOR RAID.
==

                                                          10th July 1918.
Ref. Map - 57D. S.E. 1/20,000.
1. INSTRUCTIONS.
   (a) <u>Organisation of the Party.</u> The Raiders will be divided into two
                                                parties as follows :-
                                                I. "A" Party. - on the RIGHT, Sub.Lieut
                                                BOLT in command with P.O. BESTFORD and
                                                25 O.Rs. from 13 & 14 Platoons.
                                                II. "B" Party - on the LEFT, Sub.Lieut.
                                                BRIDDON in command with P.O. NETTLESHIP
                                                and 25 O.Rs. from 15 & 16 Platoons.
   (b) <u>Assembly.</u>   Both "A" & "B" Parties will be lined
                                                up on Sunken Road with right of "A"
                                                Party at junction of Trench with road
                                                at Q.17.c.75.60. at ZERO minus 10 mins.
   (c) <u>Attack.</u>
       I. ZERO.   At ZERO hour bayonets will be fixed
                                                and both "A" & "B" Parties will then
                                                crawl forward, and get <u>close</u> behind our
                                                own barrage.
      II. <u>ZERO plus 4 mins.</u>   At ZERO plus 4 minutes, that is,
                                                immediately barrage lifts from LUSTRE
                                                SUPPORT (the 1st Objective) the whole
                                                line will charge forward and assault
                                                LUSTRE SUPPORT. This trench will be
                                                mopped up, special attention being given
                                                to Crater at Q.17.c.9.1. by "B" Party
                                                and to trench junction at Q.17.d.20.75.
                                                by "A" Party.
   (d) <u>Exploiting</u>   If at discretion of Officers on the
        <u>Success.</u>   spot success is to be exploited or if
                                                no prisoners are obtained in LUSTRE
                                                SUPPORT the parties will then proceed
                                                to the 2nd Objective, LOUNGE TRENCH.
   (e) <u>Method of Approach.</u>   I. "B" Party will leave 3 men, A.Bs.
                                                WALMESLEY, ADCOCK & MARTIN at the Crater
                                                The remainder of the party will proceed
                                                direct astride the Communication Tr.
                                                over the top to LOUNGE TRENCH except
                                                L.S. SQUIRES, A.Bs. KNOX, LOWRIE McKENZIE
                                                & BAKER who will work up Communication
                                                Trench to LOUNGE TRENCH, both parties
                                                working in conjunction with each other.
                                                On reaching LOUNGE TRENCH two men, A.Bs.
                                                FOSTER & POWELL will take up position
                                                at junction of the two trenches. The
                                                remainder of the party will work down
                                                to the right along LOUNGE TRENCH until
                                                "A" Party is met.
                                       II. "A" Party on reaching 1st Objective
                                           will send a party consisting of L.S.
                                           COOK, A.Bs. TODD, JENKINS, JONES & KIRBY
                                           along LUSTRE SUPPORT to the right for a
                                           few yards and prevent any enemy inter-
                                           fering from this trench.
                                           After "A" Party have mopped up 1st
                                           Objective it will continue at discretion
                                           of Officer on spot to LOUNGE TRENCH in
                                           following manner:- L.S. COOK, A.Bs. TODD,
                                           JENKINS, JONES & KIRBY will work along
                                           LUSTRE SUPPORT in trench to junction
                                           with LOUNGE TRENCH. All the remainder
                                           of party with the exception of A.Bs.
                                           STOCKTON, SUTHERLAND & LOGAN who will
                                           stay at 1st Objective, will proceed
                                           over the top to the 2nd Objective,
                                           when they will work to the left and
                                           get into touch with "B" Party, mopping
                                           up all along the trench.

(f) Prisoners.
After completion of mopping up, both parties will return to their own trench by the arranged route.
On prisoners being captured, men will be detailed to take same to RAID H.Qrs is rear.

(g) Signals.
When O.C., Raiding Party, Sub.Lieut.BRIDDON, thinks that the time for withdrawing has arrived, he will blow a whistle, this signal will be taken up by all the N.C.Os. The raiding force will then withdraw by the arranged route into our own lines reporting to Raid H.Qrs.

When the Raiding Force have all returned the O.C. Raid will send up the arranged rocket, which will be 3 rifle Grenade rockets bursting into two RED and two WHITE lights to signify to Artillery and M.Gs. that the raid is finished.

In addition GREEN asteroid signal rockets (50 small stars bursting into a cone) will be sent up at 3 minutes interval, commencing at ZERO plus 10 along the Front Line Trench in order to signify to raiding party the direction of our own Front Line. These lights have nothing to do with the withdrawal of the parties.

W. A. Robertson
Lieutenant R.N.V.R.,
O.C., "D" Coy.,
DRAKE Battalion.

Copies issued to :-
Copy No. 1. C.O.
2. O.C. Raid.
3. Sub.Lieut. BRIDDON.
4. Battn. Intelligence Officer.
5. 189th Infy. Brigade.
6. do.
7. do
8. 63rd (R.N) Division.
9. Sub.Lieut. BOLT.
10. P.O. "A" Party.
11. P.O. "B" Party.
12. War Diary.

SECRET.   APPENDIX "F"

63rd (RN) MACHINE GUN BATTALION OPERATION ORDER No.42.

Ref. Map.
57.D. S.E.

1. On the night 12/13th July 1918 the 189th Inf. Bde. will carry out a raid on the following objectives.-

    (a) <u>First Objective.</u> Enemy's Trench "IMSTRE SUPPORT" from Q.17.d.20.77. to Q.17.Central.

    (b) <u>Second Objective.</u> To exploit the success of (a) by clearing up "LOUNGE TRENCH" from Q.17.d.12.77 to Q.17.b.12.18.

    The raiding party will form up on track Q.17.c.75.55 to Q.17.a.6.0.

2. The following M.G. units will co-operate.-

    <u>63rd (RN) M.G. Battalion.</u>

    "A" Company   8 guns.
    "B"   "   10   "
    "C"   "   8   "
    "D"   "   12   "

    <u>38th Battalion M.G. Corps.</u>

    8 guns.

3. TASKS.

Unit.	Battery Position.	Guns.	Time.	Target.	Rate of Fire.
"A" Coy.	Trench Q.9.d.5.8.	8	ZERO to cease fire signal.	Q.17.a.55.85. to Q.18.a.5.2.	ZERO to Z plus 5 100 rounds per minute. ZERO plus 5 to Z plus 15 75 R.P.M. ZERO plus 15 onwards 100 R.P.M.
"C" Coy.	BOVET TRENCH. Q.15.a.9.9.	8	do do	Q.17.d.8.5. to Q.18.a.0.2.	do do
"B" Coy.	Trench Q.16.c.25.40.	4	do do	Q.17.d.3.2. to Q.17.d.3.5.	do do
"B" Coy.	Trench Q.15.c.9.1.	4	do do	Q.23.a.8.9. to Q.17.c.8.2.	do do

Unit.	Battery Position.	Guns.	Time.	Target.	Rate of Fire.
"B" Coy.	Q.17.a.5.1.	2	ZERO TO cease fire signal.	Q.17.b.00.25. to Q.11.b.0.6. (Flanks of Traverse).	ZERO to Z plus 5 100 rounds per min. ZERO plus 5 to Z plus 15. 75 R.P.M. ZERO plus 15½ onwards 100 R.P.M.
"D" Coy.	From vicinity of battle positions.	6	do do	Y RAVINE	do do
"D" Coy.	do do	6	do do	Q.10.b.9.0. to Q.11.a.2.6.	do do
38th Bn. M.G.C.	To be selected by O.C.38th Bn. M.G.C.	4	do do	A line Q.23.b.45.75. to Q.18.c.15.20.	do do
do do	do do	4	do do	Q.23.b.10.85. to Q.17.d.80.25.	do do

4. The G.O.C. 189th Bde. has arranged to clear the front line trench between Q.23.a.30.75. and Q.17.c.4.3.

5. All positions will be constructed during the night 11/12th July and guns will be in position by ZERO minus 2 hours.

6. Special belted ammunition will be carried in by rear details, the empty belts will be returned to Rear H.Qrs. for re-filling immediately after firing the barrage. Under no circumstances will reserves be depleted.

7. A runner will be despatched from H.Qrs. at 5.30 p.m. 12th July to synchronise watches with all units concerned.

8. Cease fire signal and ZERO HOUR will be notified all concerned in due course.

9. 63rd (RN) M.G. Companies and 38th Bn. M.G.C. to acknowledge.

Issued at 8 p.m.
10.7.18.

(sd) E. McCREADY, Lieut. Col., R.M.,
Commanding 63rd (RN) M.G. Battalion.

CONGRATULATORY WIRES - Reference Raid, 12/13th July.1918.

FROM ARMY COMMANDER :-

"Please convey my congratulations to all ranks who took part in most successful raid.

General Byng".

* * *

FROM DIVISIONAL COMMANDER :-

"Heartiest congratulations to the gallant NOVUS on their last nights complete success.

Major General LAWRIE".

* * *

FROM DIVISION ON RIGHT :- 35th Div.

"Congratulations on successful raid.

Gen. Cubitt."

* * *

From "A" and "Q" :-

"Best congratulations.

A. and Q".

* * *

Telegram of Congratulations also received from Division on Left - 42nd Div

G.O.C., ROYAL NAVAL DIVISION.

Every possible congratulation to the Division on the splendid performance by the DRAKE BATTALION of the 189th Brigade.

Will you please, when you see them, tell them from me how glad I am at their great success. The raid was a clean job, well planned, well directed, well carried out. It could not have been done better and I am sure that all concerned must be proud of it.

Many thanks to you all. Everyone will be anxious to copy you.

(sgd) C. D. SHUTE,
Lieutenant General,
Commanding, V Corps.

13th JULY 1918.

O.C., 148th Field Ambulance.

Report on German Prisoner who died at A.D. Station 13/7/18.

I beg to report that a German prisoner was brought to my Advanced Dressing Station at 5. am. yesterday. He was evidently suffering from poisoning of Phosgene Gas.

I could not get any information from him as he was in too serious a condition and did not appear to understand English.

He presented the typical signs of poisoning by Phosgene - dyapnoea, cyanosis, coughing up yellow stained frothy mucus. He died one hour after admission.

From the condition of his respirator, which contained a good deal of frothy mucus, it was evident that he had worn his respirator. This is born out by the statements of the stretcher bearers.

I cannot, however, ascertain whether he had worn his respirator before or after he had got gassed.

The presence of yellow frothy mucus in his respirator shows that serious lung symptoms had set in early.

                             (sgd)   M.A. POWER.

A.D.S.,
Mailly-Maillet.   Major, R.A.M.C.,
14./7/1918.

SECRET.   63rd (RN) Division. No.GA.5/19.

Headquarters,
V Corps.

       I have much pleasure in forwarding details of raid carried out by the DRAKE Battalion on night 12/13th July 1918.

       I concur with the able report of Commander BEAK, DRAKE Battalion, but would draw special attention to the following two points:-

(1) As on previous Divisional raids our lights failed, the remedy for this is to draw, well previous to the raid, many more lights than are necessary for the raid, so that although some may not ignite, there may be enough that will. The men too, who are told off to let these lights off during the raid, should have previous instruction in letting off the lights drawn for the raid, so that they will know what to expect.

(2) The fact that "P" bombs failed to explode I can only attribute to faulty binding in of the detonators - or to the covers of the Brock lighters on the detonators not being properly removed, and the Brock lighters not being themselves properly lit (a clumsy operation) before the bombs were thrown.

       The bombs in question (No.26) were drawn just previous to the raid from the Corps Dump, and to-day I have seen six of this same lot thrown and exploded with perfect results in each case.

       The remedy is for the raider to be properly taught in the use of the "P" bombs before the raid.

       "P" bombs No. 27 should be issued for all future raids

       The Division obtained its first actual demonstration of the effect of our own Phosgene gas, and as a matter of interest I attach report on same.

                              (sgd) C.E. LAWRIE,
                                   Major General,
15th July 1918.   Commanding, 63rd (RN) Division.

SECRET.
189th Infantry Brigade B.M.1/484
14th July 1918.

63rd (RN) Division.

Herewith report on raid of DRAKE Battalion on night 12/13th July, 1918. as under :-

(i) Report of O.C., DRAKE Battalion (in triplicate) -

    SECTION I.   General Preparation for Raid.
           II   Plan.
           III Execution.
           IV   Notes and Lessons.

(ii) Appendices (in duplicate) -

    (a) Brigade Order No. 29.
    (b) Drake Battalion Order No. 21.
        "D" Coy. Drake Battalion Order.

(iii) Maps (2 copies)

    ARTILLERY Barrage.
    MACHINE GUN Barrage.

All reports agree that the men went forward the instant the barrage opened in fine style. There was a good deal of tangled wire about and they struggled through this in a very determined way, and were into the Front trench almost as soon as the barrage lifted.

Sub.Lieut. Briddon Commanding left Party and Sub.Lieut Bolt Commanding Right Party behaved with pluck and determination. Sub.Lieut. Bolt is specially to be commended for the way he carried on and made his way into the enemy's main trench with 8 men only, thus securing the bulk of the prisoners. One of the prisoners was a fugitive from our Projector discharge on the 38th Divisional Front. He died from the effects of our gas shortly after his admission to the Dressing Station at MAILLY-MAILLET.

The "P" bombs and light signals do not appear to have been altogether satisfactory. Only 12 Asteroid signals were provided to mark our Front Line. This was not nearly enough.

The Artillery and Machine Gun barrage was everything that could be desired.

Credit is due to Lieutenant Commander Galloway, 2nd in Command and Commander Beak, Commanding DRAKE Battalion, who were in Command of the Battalion at different times during the preparation for the Careful way the preparation was carried out.

                (sgd) H. de Pree,
            Brigadier General,
     Commanding, 189th Infantry Brigade.

V CORPS. G.X.3908.

A particularly successful raid, carried out with determination and great fighting spirit. It is a pity more rifles, M.G. Belts, Ammunition, &c., are not brought back on these occasions, but in this raid the party was a small one.

Great credit is due to those who planned and organised the raid.

(sgd) C.D. SHUTE, Lt-General,
Commanding V CORPS.

16/7/1918.

Third Army No.G.12/280.

G.O.C., V Corps.

Reference your G.X. 3908 of 16th inst.
This was a most successful exploit, well planned, and rehearsed and well executed.
It reflects very great credit on the organizers and raiders.

18/7/1918.   (sgd)   J. BYNG, General.

V CORPS.

G.X. 3908.
19th July 1918.

63rd DIVISION.

Please see the above remarks by the Army Commander and Corps Commander on the raid carried out by the "DRAKE" Battalion on night of 12th/13th inst.

(sgd) R.H. MANGLES,
B. G., G.S.
V CORPS.

63rd (R.N) Division. No.GA.5/19.

189th INFANTRY BRIGADE.

The above remarks by Army and Corps Commanders are forwarded for information, together with a copy of the Divisional Commanders remarks on the raid, forwarded under 63rd Divisional No. G.A.5/19, dated 15th July.

(sgd) M. Soutry.
Lieutenant Colonel,
General Staff,
63rd (RN) Division.

20th July 1918.

Appendix 'B'

SECRET.

COPY No. ...

Headquarters, 189th Infantry Brigade.

10th July, 1918.

189th INFANTRY BRIGADE ORDER NO. 29.

Ref. Map,
57d.S.E.,1/20,000.

1. The Drake Battalion will carry out a raid on the enemy's trenches at ZERO HOUR on the night 12th/13th July 1918 with the object of :-

    (a)   Capturing and killing as many of the enemy as possible.

    (b)   Obtaining identifications and documents.

    (c)   Capturing Machine Guns and destroying dugouts and shelters in the area raided.

2. OBJECTIVES.

    (a) First Objective - Enemy's trench, "LUSTRE SUPPORT" from Q.17.d.20.77 - Q.17.central.

    (b) Second Objective - To exploit success of (a) by clearing up "LOUNGE TRENCH" from Q.17.d.42.77 - Q.17.b.12.18

3. STRENGTH OF RAIDING PARTY.

    1 Officer as O.C. Raid, and 2 Officers and 52 O.Rs.

4. ZERO HOUR.

    Will be notified later to all concerned.

5. ARTILLERY, TRENCH MORTARS & M.G. SUPPORT.

    Is being arranged.   Details will be notified later to those concerned.

6. SIGNALS.

(a) O.C. Raid will send up three Rifle Grenade Rockets bursting into two RED and two WHITE Lights from the Front Line at Q.17.a.6.1 as a signal to the Artillery and Machine Guns that the raiding party has returned, and that the protective barrage can cease.

2.

(6) "O.C. Raid will arrange to send up from different points in the Front Line between Q.17.a.5.3 and Q.17.c.5.0 a series of GREEN asteroid signal rockets (50 small stars bursting into a cone) from ZERO plus 6 minutes till the raiding party returns, to indicate to the raiding party the position of our line."

7. The Brigade Signal Officer will arrange to connect up the Headquarters of O.C. Raid with Front Battalion Headquarters by Fullerphone.

8. The Brigade Intelligence Officer will synchronize watches at Headquarters Front Battalion at 7-30 pm, 12th July with the following :-

    Drake Battalion
    189th Stokes T.M.Battery

9. O.C., Drake Battalion will forward three copies of his detail orders for the raid to Brigade Headquarters by 11th July.

10. ACKNOWLEDGE.

        Captain,
    Brigade Major, 189th Infantry Brigade.

Issued through Signals to :-

  Copy No. 1. Drake Battalion
     2. Hawke "
     3. Hood "
     4. 189th Stokes T.M.Bty.
     5. 63rd (RN) Division "G"
     6. 63rd (RN) Divisional Artillery
     7. 223rd Brigade R.F.A.
     8. 188th Infantry Brigade
     9. 190th " "
    10. 115th " "
    11. 63rd (RN) Machine Gun Battalion

SECRET.

189th Infantry Brigade.B.M.1/442/1.

11th July, 1918.

Reference para. 5 of 189th Infantry Brigade Order No. 29, of 10/7/18.

1. Herewith Tables showing action of

"A" 18 pounders
"B" 4.5" Howitzers
"C" 6" Newton Trench Mortars
"D" 3" Stokes Mortars
"E" Machine Gun Barrage

2. In addition Heavy Artillery are engaging suitable targets and carrying out counter battery work.

3. ACKNOWLEDGE.

Captain,
Brigade Major, 189th Infantry Brigade.

Issued through Signals at 6-30 pm., 11/7/18 to :-

Drake Battalion
Hawke   "
Hood   "
189th Stokes T.M.Bty.
63rd (RN) Division "G"
63rd (RN) Divisional Artillery
115th Infantry Brigade.

TABLE "A". 18 Pounders. (To accompany 189th Infantry Brigade Order No. 29.)

UNIT.	TIME.	TASK.	RATE. R.p.g.p.m.	REMARKS.
C/223 A/223 B/232 (4 guns)	Zero to Zero plus 4'.	Q.17.b.12.18 - Q.17.a.98.02 Q.17.a.98.02 - Q.17.d.14.80 Q.17.d.14.80 - Q.17.d.38.78	3.	(Lifting Barrage opens on dotted (GREEN LINE. ((All shrapnel.
C/225 A/225 B/232 (4 guns)	Zero plus 4' to "Cease Fire"	Q.17.b.00.43 - Q.17.b.25.57 Q.17.b.42.30 - Q.17.b.68.12 Q.17.d.38.54 - Q.17.d.75.45	2.	(Barrage lifts from dotted GREEN (LINE on to GREEN Line½ (All H.E. 101 fuze.
B/317 C/317 B/232 (3 guns) A/232 (2 guns) A/232 (4 guns)	Zero to Zero plus 5'.	Q.17.b.00.43 - Q.17.b.20.12 Q.17.b.20.12 - Q.17.d.37.78 Q.17.d.37.78 - C.17.d.54.53 Q.17.b.20.12 - Q.17.b.42.14 Q.17.d.37.77 - Q.17.d.77.61	3.	(Lifting Barrage opens on dotted (YELLOW LINE. (All shrapnel.
B/317 C/317 B/232 (2 guns) A/232 (6 guns)	Zero plus 5' to "Cease Fire".	Q.17.b.25.57 - Q.17.b.42.30 Q.17.b.68.12 - Q.17.d.76.81 Q.17.d.38.54 - Q.17.d.75.45 Q.17.d.76.81 - Q.17.d.75.45	2.	(Barrage lifts from dotted YELLOW (to the YELLOW Line. (All H.E. 101 fuze. delay.
C/232 A/317 B/223	Zero to "Cease Fire".	Q.17.d.38.54 - Q.17.d.75.44 Q.17.d.38.54 - Q.17.d.44.18 Q.17.d.86.16 - Q.17.d.00.52 Q.17.d.27.15	Z to Z plus 5'- 3. Z plus 5' onwards - 2.	(Standing Barrage opens on BLUE LINE. (All shrapnel except C/232, which (will fire H.E. 101 fuze delay.

TABLE "A" (continued)

UNIT.	TIME.	TASK.	RATE. R.p.g.p.m.	REMARKS.
3-18 pdr. Batts. 42nd D.A.	Zero to "Cease Fire".	Q.4.d.7.8 - Q.5.c.00.48 - Q.10.b.84.86.	Z to Z plus 5' -2. Z plus 5' to "Cease Fire" - 1	(Standing Barrage to divert (attention from Front raided.
38th D.A. 1-18 pdr. Bty.	do.	Q.17.d.45.18 - Q.23.b.57.85	Z to Z plus 5' - 3.	Standing Barrage. All shrapnel
1-18 pdr. Bty.		Q.17.d.03.02 - Q.17.d.27.02 - Q.23.b.45.90.		
1-18 pdr. Bty.		Q.23.b.45.90 - Q.23.b.73.67	Z plus 5' to "Cease Fire" - 2.	
1-18 pdr. (3 guns) Bty. (5 guns)		Q.17.d.27.15 - Q.17.d.45.18 Q.23.b.73.67 - Q.23.b.86.83		

TABLE "B". 4.5" Hows. (To accompany 189th Infantry Brigade Order No. 29.)

UNIT.	TIME.	TASK.	RATE. R.P.G.p.m.	REMARKS.
D/223 (4 guns)	Zero to Zero plus 4'.	Q.17.b.30.15. Q.17.b.42.15. Q.17.d.52.70. Q.17.d.70.65.	2.	All EX.101 fuze only.
D/223 (4 guns)	Zero plus 4' to "Cease Fire".	Q.17.b.45.56. Q.17.b.58.62. Q.17.b.66.27. Q.17.b.96.06.	1.	ditto.
D/232 D/317 D/223 (2 guns)	Zero to "Cease Fire".	Q.11.c.60.23 – Q.17.a.86.82 Q.17.a.86.82 – Q.17.b.00.42 Q.17.d.74.35.– Q.17.d.80.35.	Z to Z plus 6'- 2. Z plus 6' to "Cease Fire" – 1.	ditto.
1 Bty. 38th D.A.	Zero to "Cease Fire".	Q.17.d.83.28 – Q.23.b.88.88	Z to Z plus 6'- 2 Z plus 6' to "Cease Fire" – 1.	ditto.

TABLE "C". 6" Trench Mortars. (To accompany 189th Infantry Brigade Order No. 29.)

	TIME.	TASK.	RATE. R.P.G.P.m.
4 - 6" Trench Mortars.	Zero to "Cease Fire"	Q.11.c.5.5 Q.17.a.85.83 Q.17.a.95.58 Q.17.d.05.03	Zero to Zero plus 5': - 2. 6' Zero plus 5' to Cease Fire": - 1.

TABLE "D" - Action of 189th Stokes Mortar Battery- to accompany 189th Infantry Brigade Order No.29.

NUMBER of MORTARS.	TARGET.	REMARKS.
5.	LUSTRE SUPPORT from Q.17.a.99.02 - Q.17.d.40.78)) New Trench - Q.17.b.10.10.)	To fire from Zero to Zero plus 3' - Rapid fire-20 rounds p.g.p.m.
2.	LOUNGE TRENCH from Q.17.b.12.20 - Q.17.b.42.78)	To fire from Zero to Zero plus 4' - Rapid fire - 20 rounds p.g.p.m.

H.Q., 189th Stokes T.M.Bty. will be established with Drake Battalion Forward H.Q. in Locality No. 4 - Q.16.b.2.5 by Zero minus one hour.

TABLE "E" - Machine Gun Barrage. (To accompany 189th Infantry Brigade Order No. 29.

UNIT.	BATTERY POSITION.	GUNS.	Time.	TARGET.	RATE OF FIRE.
"A" Coy.	Trench Q.9.d.5.8.	8	Zero to "Cease Fire" signal.	Q.17.a.55.85 to Q.18.a.5.2.	Zero to Zero plus 5' 100 rounds per min. Zero plus 5' to Zero plus 15', 75 r.p.m. Zero plus 15' onwards, 100 r.p.m.
"C" Coy.	BOVET TRENCH Q.15.a.9.9.	8	do.	Q.17.d.8.5 to Q.18.a.0.2.	do.
"B" Coy.	Trench Q.16.c.25.40	4	do.	Q.17.d.3.2 to Q.17.d.3.5.	do.
"B" Coy.	Trench Q.15.c.9.1.	4	do.	Q.23.a.8.9 to Q.17.c.8.2.	do.
"B" Coy.	Q.17.a.5.1.	2	do.	Q.17.b.00.25 to Q.11.b.0.6 (Flankless of Traverse).	do.
"D" Coy.	From vicinity of Battle Positions.	6	do.	"Y" Ravine	do.
"D" Coy.	Vicinity do.	6	do.	Q.10.b.0.9 to Q.11.a.2.6.	do.
38th Bn. M.G.C.	To be selected by O.C.,38th Bn.M.G.C.	4	do.	A line Q.23.b.45.75 to Q.18.c.15.20.	do.
do.	do.	4	do.	Q.23.b.10.65 to Q.17.d.80.25.	do.

REPORT ON RAID CARRIED OUT BY DRAKE BATTALION ON 12th/13th JULY ON MAILLY RIGHT SECTOR.

SECTION I.   **GENERAL PREPARATION FOR THE RAID.**

The first intimation that a raid was to be carried out was received on June 30th 1918 while the Battalion was holding the Advanced Forward Zone. Very active patrolling was immediately instituted in addition to the normal patrols in order to discover a suitable portion of the enemy's line to raid.

(a) **Reason for selection of position raided.**

Enemy position opposite Left of Battalion Sector was denied to us owing to Brigade on the Left carrying out a raid in this vicinity. Information was obtained by patrols that the enemy had a post in crater at Q.17.a.95.05 as Very lights were continually being sent up from this point, and our patrols always encountered machine gun fire from the same point. A post was also discovered on the Right of the Battalion Front at Q.17.d.1.1. After due consideration it was decided that the post in the crater at Q.17.a.95.05 was more suitable to raid for the following reasons :-

(1) Less wire in front of SOUTH-WEST face.
(2) It was considered that rushing the post from the SOUTH-WEST would be in the nature of a surprise as the enemy appeared to anticipate trouble from the direction of locality A.7. which is due WEST from the post. This was assumed from the fact that most of his sniping from this post was in that direction, and also the wire on the WEST and NORTH-WEST face of the post was very thick.

(b) **Wire cutting.**

Destructive shoots were carried out on the wire on the following dates :-

(1) July 5th
(2) July 10th
(3) July 11th

Battalion in the line was asked to prevent repair by the enemy of any gaps made by these shoots by keeping up short bursts of Lewis gun fire on the gaps throughout the nights.

The wire in front of the SOUTH-WEST face of the objective was mostly of the barbed concertina pattern and included both old and new wire which, (as far as could be ascertained by ground observation) appeared to be very insecurely staked to the ground. Patrol reconnaissance confirmed this.

On the 12th instant final observation of the wire showed it to be broken in many places and it was decided that further shooting should not be carried out as existing wire did not seem a big obstacle, also the raid carried out on our Right on the night of the 11th/12th would assist in making our raid the following night more of a surprise to the enemy and should wire-cutting take place on the 12th, this might tend to take away the element of surprise thus gained and place the enemy on the alert.

(c) **Patrolling.**

The two Officers of the raiding party, the Battalion I.O. and all N.C.Os of raiding parties reconnoitred the approaches to and the trenches in the vicinity of the position on four separate occasions; in addition at least half of the men went out also to reconnoitre in small parties with N.C.Os. The remainder all viewed the objectives from our own Front Line.

(d) **Raid Practice.**

On the night of 5th/6th July the Battalion was relieved from Front Line and went into Reserve. Two models of the course, one miniature and one full size, were laid out and completed by the 7th instant. The raiding parties were first taken over the miniature course several times, and details of the trenches and also of each man's own particular job in the raid pointed out to him. The men then went over the full sized course several times as a drill in slow time, mistakes were corrected and the actual positions given to the men. They then practised several times as a "real show" with drums and tins to simulate a barrage. A miniature of the course was then drawn on a waterproof sheet showing route out to Assembly Position, Assembly Position, trenches to be crossed, position of wire, flanks of attack, actual objectives and route to return. Each party was then lectured by its own Officer on its own particular work and positions and on the raid as a whole. They were then lectured by O.C. raid and O.C. Battalion. G.O.C., 189th Infantry Brigade talked to the men on their duties and this was followed by a further talk by G.O.C., (RN) Division on the objects of the raid and special points to be remembered. The spirit of the men was splendid and great keenness was shown throughout all the practises.

SECTION II.   **GENERAL PLAN OF RAID.**

The general idea of the scheme was

(1) To assault LUSTRE SUPPORT from Q.17.d.2.7 to crater at Q.17.central paying special attention to crater which was believed to be the only portion of this first objective which was occupied by the enemy.

(2) To exploit success and clear up LOUNGE TRENCH from Q.17.d.4.7 to Q.17.d.1.2 where dugouts were believed to exist.

(a) **Method of attack.**

It was considered that two Officers, two P.Os., and fifty O.Rs. were sufficient for the work; they were divided equally into two parties known respectively as "A" Party and "B" Party.

(1) "A" Party of one Officer, one P.O. and 25 O.Rs. was to be responsible for the Right half of the first objective, the party then to continue to known post at junction of LOUNGE TRENCH and LUSTRE SUPPORT at Q.17.d.4.7 in the following manner :- Four men working up LUSTRE SUPPORT inside trench, the remainder going astride the trench over the top. Three men of this party were to be left behind at the first objective to mop up.

(2) "B" Party of 1 Officer, 1 P.O. & 25 O.Rs to be responsible for the Left Half of the first objective, paying particular attention to the Crater at Q.17. central, party then to continue to 2nd objective in the following manner:- Four men to work up Communication Trench to LOUNGE TRENCH at Q.17.b.1.2. and the remainder of the party astride the Communication Trench over the top. Three men of this party were to be left in the Crater to mop up.

Both parties on reaching the 2nd Objective were to mop up LOUNGE Trench, "A" party working to the left and "B" party working to the right until both met when they were to return to their own front line by arranged route.

(b) **Signals.**

(i) For actual return of party by means of blasts on whistle.

(ii) In order to indicate the direction of our own front line to the raiding parties, GREEN Lights were to be sent up at pre-arranged intervals.

(iii) For barrage to cease, ROCKETS of a pre-arranged colour were to be sent up.

SECTION III. **EXECUTION OF RAID.**

On account of the muddy condition of the trenches caused by the rain of the previous day, it was considered necessary to move up to the line at ZERO minus 3 hours instead of ZERO minus 2½ hours. The raiding parties arrived in the Front Line well up to time and hot tea and meat sandwiches were issued to each raider. Punctually at ZERO minus 45 minutes after they had had a rest of an hour and a quarter in the Front Line, they started out to form up in the Assembly Position. The spacing out of the men was excellently arranged by the Officers responsible and the whole raiding party was in position at ZERO minus 15 minutes without a hitch. The barrage opened right on the second and every man automatically fixed bayonets and walked up to within 30 yards of the barrage. The line moved forward splendidly just as if they were on parade. At ZERO plus 3 minutes the party arrived at the wire which, despite a few gaps, caused some difficulty. The men persevered and won their way through the wire and charged the first objective with a lusty cheer. It was noted that the wire was loosely and sparingly staked and although a fair height it was kept down fairly easily by stepping on the centre of the concertina between the stakes.

When "B" Party on the Left arrived at the crater they found the Bosche 'standing to' and he immediately began to show opposition. Some of the Bosche were on the fire-step and some were in the trench. They refused to surrender and showed resistance, consequently they were killed. In the trench the party found 3 dugout entrances on each side; a number of Bosche found on the steps of the entrances showed fight, they refused to come out and "P" bombs followed by Mills grenades were thrown down the entrances. It is absolutely certain that the occupants were killed. Every dugout entrance encountered, whether containing visible occupants or not, was treated in a similar manner; one dugout was actually in flames before the party left.

The party then moved forward as arranged and then along LOUNGE TRENCH until "A" Party was met. A Bosche was found in LOUNGE TRENCH in the act of firing a light machine gun. He refused to surrender and tries to turn the gun on the party. The Officer in charge of the party killed him with his revolver and captured the gun. Another Bosche was found in the act of firing his rifle ; he was overpowered and taken prisoner and sent to Raid H.Q. making two attempts to escape on his way there. All the Bosche actually killed by this party in the trenches were searched before being left, but nothing was found on any of them, the only things found on this one prisoner were a purse and identity disc.

The Officer in charge of "B" Party continued the search but without further success and evntually withdrew his party to our lines at ZERO plus 65 minutes.

"A" Party on the Right on reaching their first objective found nothing in the trench. They then continued half right over the top to LOUNGE TRENCH ; a bombing party working up LUSTRE SUPPORT met with opposition and were bombed. The rest of the party on arriving at their second objective immediately met one Bosche, who called down a dugout and 2 or 3 others came out and surrendered. The party then worked along the trench and found 12 dugout entrances. The inmates were called upon to surrender which they did without resistance. "P" bombs were flung down all these entrances after the prisoners had come out, but on account of the number of "P" bombs failing to explode, Mills bombs were thrown down afterwards but the latter were not sufficient to burn the dugout. In this vicinity "A" Party captured altogether 21 prisoners and 1 heavy machine gun which was destroyed. The Officer in charge and 7 men of the party were responsible for the actual capture of these men. There were more Bosche in the partof the line "A" Party raided, but they were killed, and the Officer in charge returned to our own lines with his captives at ZERO plus 45 minutes.

<u>Our Artillery and Machine Gun Support.</u>

The barrage put up by our Artillery was excellent being exceptionally clean.

The machine gun barrage must also have been very effective if any of the enemy tried to escape over the open.

<u>Particulars re Enemy Trenches.</u>

The trenches were about 9 feet deep and well dug; they were in a good and fairly dry condition but n o duck-boards or revetments were observed. The dugouts appeared to be deep with numerous well constructed entrances. All fire positions seemed to be in small cuts into the parapet just large enough to hold one man, and in many of these small positions one rifle was seen, but none with fixed bayonets. At the crater on the Left a machine gun emplacement with several boxes of ammunition and belts was found but no gun could be seen. The wire in front of the enemy lines was fairly thick and formed a bigger obstacle than had been anticipated.

<u>Enemy Retaliation.</u>

At about ZERO plus 30, enemy trench mortars crumped their own Front Line including the raided area but fortunately this did not affect the progress of the raid. Most of his artillery retaliation, which commenced about ZERO plus 15 minutes appeared to be placed on the MESNIL Sector, though a few crumps came into EATON LANE.

Lights.

(a) **Enemy.** Only a few lights were put up, mainly orange, with a few reds.

(b) **Ours.** The GREEN asteroid lights quite failed to fulfill their purpose : instead of bursting into a great number of Green stars as expected they assumed various forms. Five out of the twelve were "duds".

The rockets for the "Cease Barrage" signal served their purpose quite well, but three out of the seven rockets were "duds".

The enemy lights were markedly superior to ours in every way.

Result of Raid.

Enemy Casualties.

Prisoners 23
Machine Guns captured 2
(including 1 heavy gun destroyed and left in "No Mans Land").
Enemy killed (actually seen dead) 7.
Enemy believed killed and wounded at least 20.

Dugouts.

18 entrances bombed and 1 dugout actually left burning.

Rifles.

Several rifles were taken out of the enemy trenches but owing to difficulties encountered on way back only two are now actually in our possession.

Our Own casualties.

Wounded. 5 O.Rs.
Missing 1 O.R.

SECTION IV. **LESSONS LEARNED FROM RAID.**

(a) For complete success it is essential that a raid be not rushed upon a Battalion but sufficient notice given to allow time for the following :-
 (i) Active patrolling by the raiders, of the area selected for the raid.
 (ii) Practice on a full size course.
 (iii) Opportunity of getting all the raiders together for intimate talks on the subject, illustrated by diagrams. This point is considered to be a most important one and cannot be too strongly emphasised.

As a result of having the above privileges all reports of the raid show that each man knew his own particular job, and that the whole operation was carried out with drill-like precision.

(b) It is considered that the Officers in charge of the raiding parties, althogugh receiving definite and detailed orders for each minute particular, should not however be tied down too strictly, in exploiting success. They should be fully trusted to use their initiative within certain bounds, and it should be made quite clear to them that upon their leadership and judgement depends the success of the operation.

(c) In the talks to the men great stress should be laid on their vast superiority man to man over the Bosche, and every effort made to work upon the men's enthusiasm.

(d) As far as we know the operation was carried out exactly as practised on the taped out course, except that one Officer and seven O.Rs. with prisoners came back by a route other than that pre-arranged.

In conclusion it is felt that the greatest credit reflects upon the two Officers and the men of the raiding parties for the grim determination which they displayed in carrying out the object of the raid.

                 (sd) D.M.W. BEAK,
                       Commander, R.N.V.R.
                       Commanding Drake Battalion.

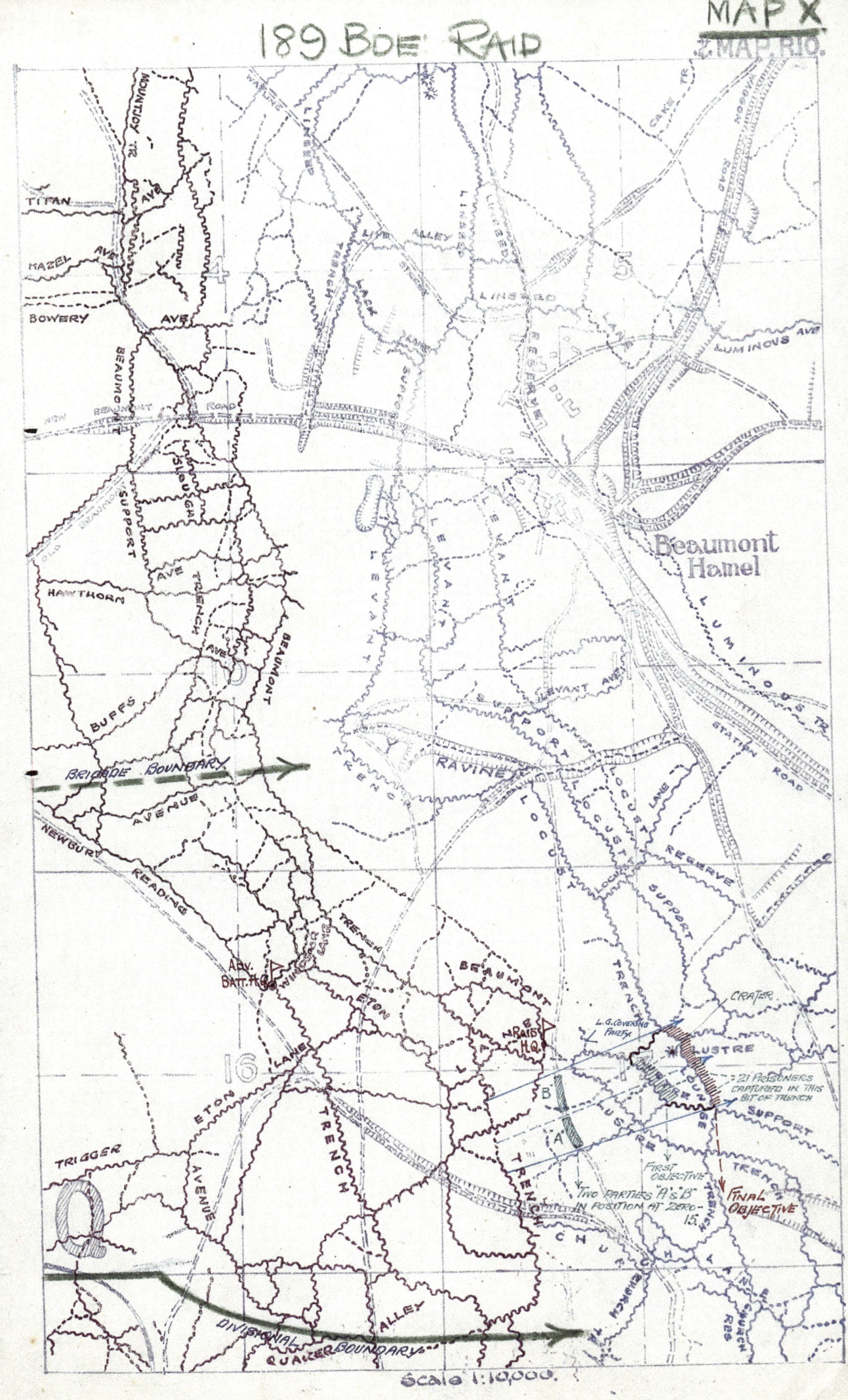

TABLE "A". 18 Pounders.(To accompany 33rd (R.N.) D.A.Operation Order No.204).

UNIT.	TIME.	TASK.	RATE. r.p.g.p.m.	REMARKS.
C/223.	Zero to Zero plus 4'.	Q.17.b.12.13. - Q.17.a.98.02.	3.	Lifting Barrage opens on dotted GREEN LINE.
A/223. B/232. (4 guns)	" "	Q.17.a.98.02. - Q.17.a.14.80. Q.17.d.14.80. - Q.17.d.38.78.		All shrapnel.
C/223. A/223. B/232. (4 guns)	Zero plus 4' to "Cease Fire."	Q.17.b.00.43. - Q.17.b.23.57. Q.17.b.43.30. - Q.17.b.68.12. Q.17.d.38.54. - Q.17.d.75.45.	2.	Barrage lifts from dotted GREEN LINE on to GREEN Line. All H.E. 101 fuze.
B/317. C/317. B/232. (2 guns)	Zero to Zero plus 6'.	Q.17.b.00.43. - Q.17.b.20.12. Q.17.b.20.12. - Q.17.d.37.73. Q.17.d.37.73. - Q.17.d.54.53.	3.	Lifting Barrage opens on dotted YELLOW LINE. All shrapnel.
A/232. (2 guns)	"	Q.17.b.20.12. - Q.17.b.42.14.		
A/232. (4 guns)	"	Q.17.d.57.77. - Q.17.d.77.61.		
B/317. C/317. B/232. (2 guns)	Zero plus 6' to "Cease fire."	Q.17.b.35.57. - Q.17.b.42.30. Q.17.b.68.12. - Q.17.d.76.81. Q.17.d.38.54. - Q.17.d.75.45.	2.	Barrage lifts from dotted YELLOW to the YELLOW Line. All H.E. 101 fuze.delay.
A/232. (3 guns)	"	Q.17.d.73.81. - Q.17.d.75.45.		
C/232. A/317. B/223.	Zero to "Cease Fire."	Q.17.d.38.54.-Q.17.d.75.44. Q.17.d.38.54.-Q.17.d.44.18. Q.17.c.86.13.-Q.17.d.00.32.-- Q.17.d.27.15.	Z to Z +5' - 3. Z +5' onwards - 2.	Standing Barrage opens on BLUE LINE. All shrapnel except C/232,which will fire H.E. 101 fuze delay.

TABLE "A".(contd)

- 2 -

UNIT.	TIME.	TASK.	RATE. R.p.g.p.m.	REMARKS.
3-18 pdr. Batts.42nd D.A.	Zero to "Cease Fire."	Q.4.d.7.8.-Q.5.c.00.48.- Q.10.b.8.86.	Z to Z + 5:- 2. Z + 6:- Z + 6" to "Cease Fire" - 1.	Standing Barrage to divert attention from front raided.
38th D.A. 1-18 pdr. Bty.	-do-	Q.17.d.45.18.-Q.25.b.57.85.	Z to Z + 6":- 3.	Standing Barrage. All shrapnel.
1-18 pdr. Bty.		Q.17.c.05.03.-Q.17.d.27.03.- Q.33.b.45.90.	Z + 6" to "Cease Fire" - 2.	
1-18 pdr. Bty.		Q.23.b.45.90.-Q.23.b.73.67.		
1-18 pr.(3 guns) Bty. (3 guns)		Q.17.d.27.15.-Q.17.d.45.18. Q.23.b.73.67.-Q.23.b.83.85.		

TABLE "B". 4.5" Hows. (To accompany 33rd (R.N.) D.A. Operation Order No.204).

UNIT.	TIME.	TASK.	RATE. P.D.P.M.	REMARKS.
D/223. (4 guns)	Zero to Zero plus 4'.	Q.17.b.50.13. Q.17.b.42.13. Q.17.c.52.70. Q.17.d.70.35.	2.	All EX.101 fuze only.
D/223. (4 guns)	Zero plus 4' to "Cease Fire."	Q.17.b.46.56. Q.17.b.53.62. Q.17.b.83.27. Q.17.b.95.06.	1.	-ditto-
D/252. D/517. D/223. (2 guns)	Zero to "Cease Fire."	Q.11.c.80.23.-Q.17.a.83.82. Q.17.a.83.82.-Q.17.b.00.43. Q.17.d.74.55.-Q.17.d.80.55.	Z to Z + 6 :- 2. Z +6' to "Cease Fire" :- 1.	-ditto-
1 Bty. 38th D.A.	Zero to "Cease Fire."	Q.17.d.85.28.-Q.23.b.83.12.	Z to Z +6' :- 2. Z +6' to "Cease Fire" :- 1.	-ditto-
1 Bty. 38th D.A.	Zero to "Cease Fire"	R.13.c.00.15. - R.13.c.50.90.	Z to Z plus 6:- 2. Zero plus 6 to "Cease Fire".	"BX" .106 fuze. Search up & down trench.

TABLE "C". 8" Trench Mortars. (To accompany 83rd (E.M.) D.A.Operation Order No.204).

TIME.	TASK.	RATE. R.P.G.P.M.

4 - 8" Trench Mortars.   Zero to "Cease Fire."   Q.11.c.5.5.   Zero to Zero plus 5'6':- 2.
                                                 Q.17.a.85.83.
                                                 Q.17.a.95.58.   Zero plus 5'6' to "Cease Fire":- 1.
                                                 Q.17.d.05.03.

APPENDIX No. II.

To be read in conjunction with Operation Order No. 21

MEDICAL ARRANGEMENTS.

BEARER POST. 1.   6 Stretchers bearers and 3 stretchers will be established at Battle H.Qrs.

AID POSTS. 2.   The Battalion Medical Officer, Medical Corporal, 6 Stretcher Bearers and 3 Stretchers will be established at Forward Battalion Headquarters.

All Stretcher cases and walking cases will return via A 7 Locality ETON LANE.

APPENDIX. No. III.

To be read in conjunction with Operation Order No 21.

SIGNAL ARRANGEMNTS.

Communication will be established between Battle H.Qrs and Forward Battalion H.Qrs by Fullerphone by 6.00.p.m. on 12th inst.

The following code will be used in sending messages to Brigade Headquarters, and signal forms will be made out ready for transmission as the times are reported to O.C. Raid.

MESSAGE.	CODE.	TIME.
Raiding Party arrived in Front Line.	"DOOR" ✓	....
Raiding party starting from Q.17.c.4.4.	"WINDOW" ✓	....
Covering party in position.	"ROOM" ✓	....
Raiding party in position.	"KITCHEN" ✓	....
Raid Started	"TABLE" ✓	....
Raiding party returned.	"CHAIR"	....
Covering Party returned.	"SOFA"	....

FINAL MESSAGE - Result of raid in clear.

When Battle H.Qrs are being vacated after the raid, the fullerphone will be disconnected and brought back by the Signallers to the Reserve position.

APPENDIX No. I.

To be read in conjunction with Operation Order No. 21.

DRESS. 1. Rifle, Bayonet & Bandolier, ~~Skeleton Order~~, Steel Helmets, S.B.Rs, Field Dressings and Special Identity Discs. Every man will carry two bombs, one in each bottom tunic pocket. In addition 16 "P" Bombs will be carried, which will be equally distributed, and also 20 Rifle Grenades.

All Numerals, badges, identity discs, paybooks, private correspondence, and any other means of identification will be packed in the Haversack, which will be stored under guard at Coy H.Q.

Officers - Equipment as above, but will carry revolvers.

MEALS. 2. The Q.M. will arrange for extra rations to be issued to O.C. "D" Coy in order that the raiding party may receive a hot meal before proceeding forward.

An extra tea, milk and sugar ration will also be issued to O.C. "D" Coy, who will detail 1 Cook and a carrying party to take up to the Right Forward Coy Cook-house all the necessary gear (including drinking vessels) required for the preparation of tea.

Every man will receive one pint of tea before ZERO minus 45 minutes.

After completion of raid and party have returned to Coy Area a rum ration will be issued to all ratings.

SECRET.
Copy No...9...

SCHEME FOR RAID BY "DRAKE" BATTALION
on the night of 12th/13th. July. 1918.

Ref. Map 57d. S.E. 1/20,000.

1. **OBJECTIVE.**   To raid LUSTRE SUPPORT from Q.17.a.90.05. to Q.17.d.2.7.

2. **OBJECT.**
   - (a) To obtain identification re prisoners, maps, &c.
   - (b) To demolish enemy defence works.
   - (c) To exploit success.

3. **STRENGTH.**   2 Officers, 2 P.Os. & 50 O.Rs., also covering party of 1 Lewis Gun Section, (1 N.C.O. & 6 O.Rs.)

4. **O.C., RAID.**   Lieut. W.A. ROBERTSON. M.C.

5. **METHOD OF ATTACK.**   The Raiding Party will leave trench at Q.17.C.4.4. and will be lined up with the right on Q.17.d.0.3. and the left on Q.17.C.75.90., under the supervision of the Battalion Intelligence Officer who will report them in position by runner to O.C., RAID at Battle H.Q. by ZERO - 10 minutes.
   On barrage lifting from LUSTRE SUPPORT, the raiding party will move forward and rush enemy position. Parties will be specially told off for the following duties:-
   - (a) A blocking party will establish themselves at Q.17.d.25.70. for the purpose of making the right flank secure.
   - (b) For dealing with enemy post in Crater at Q.17.a.95.05.
   - (c) To exploit success by moving forward along new trench leading from above Crater to LOCUST TRENCH at Q.17.d.15.20.

6. **CO-OPERATION.**   Artillery, Trench Mortar and Machine Gun Co-operation is being arranged.

7. **DRESS.**   Skeleton Order, Steel Helmets, S.B.Rs., Field Dressings and special Identity Discs. Every man will carry two bombs (one in each bottom tunic pocket)
   All numerals, badges, Identity Discs, Pay books, private correspondence and any other means of identification, will be packed in the man's haversack which will be stacked at the reserve position.

8. **WITHDRAWAL.**   The signal for the withdrawal will be arranged later.

9. **ROUTE OF WITHDRAWAL.**   The raiding party will return via the old trench at Q.17.a.95.05. to A.7 locality at Q.17.a.6.1. where they will report at Battle H.Q. to O.C., RAID.
   The withdrawal will be covered by L.G. Section established in the old trench at Q.17.a.75.15.

10. **TERMINATING SIGNAL.**   A rocket light signal, - Colours to be arranged later - will be fired from A.7. locality to signify the termination of the raid.

11. **BEARER POST.**   The bearer post will consist of six bearers with 3 stretchers, who will be located at Battle H.Q.

12. **FORWARD BATTN. H.Q.**   These will be established at Q.16.B.2.5. in A.4. locality.

D. Galloway.
Lieut. Commander. R.N.V.R.,
DRAKE Battalion.

Appendix C

SECRET.   Copy No. 14

DRAKE BATTALION OPERATION ORDER No. 21.

Reference map- Sheet 57D S.E. 1/20,000.   8th July 1918.

INTENTION	1.	"D" Coy will carry out a raid on the night 12/13 inst., on the Brigade Front. ZERO hour to be notified later.
OBJECTIVE	2.	To raid LUSTRE SUPPORT Trench from Q.17.d.2.7. to Crater at Q.17.central. If no prisoners are taken in this or if the Officer on the spot thinks the enemy are demoralised, to continue the attack and clear up LOUNGE TRENCH from Q.17.d.4.7. to Q.17.b.1.2.
OBJECT.	3.	(a) To obtain identification i.e. prisoners, documents etc. (b) To put as large a number as possible of the enemy out of action. (c) To demolish dugouts, capture arms etc.
STRENGTH.	4.	Raiding Party of 2 Officers, 2 P.Os, and 50 O.Rs. which will be organised as follows:- "A" Party - Sub.Lieut BOLT, 1 P.O. and 25 O.Rs. "B" " - Sub.Lieut BRIDDON (O.C.Raiding Party) 1 P.O. and 25 O.Rs. Covering Party (Lewis Gun) - 1 N.C.O. & 6 O.Rs.
O.C.RAID.	5.	Lieut W.A.ROBERTSON M.C. who will establish his Battle H.Q in dugout in BEAUMONT Trench at approximately Q.17.a.6.1. by ZERO minus 1 hour, accompanied by his Battle H.Q. personnel,viz:- 2 Sigs, 2 Runners, 6 Stretcher Bearers and 3 Stretchers.
O.C.RAIDING PARTY.	6.	Sub.Lieut H.B.BRIDDON R.N.V.R.
Officer i/c FORMING UP.	7.	The Battalion Intelligence Officer, Sub.Lieut S.V.G. WALKER M.M. accompanied by 3 Runners from Battalion H.Qrs
COVERING PARTY.	8.	Sub.Lieut G.HUNTER accompanied by 1 Runner from "C" Coy will be responsible for placing the Covering Party of One Lewis Gun Section in position, in the old Trench at Q.17.a. 75.15. He will report to Battle H.Qrs that this has been done by ZERO minus 10 minutes. In addition he is respon--sible for the return of the Covering Party at the conclusion of the raid.
PRELIMINARY DISPOSITIONS	9.	At ZERO minus 2½ hours. The party will move off from the Support position in the following order at 3 minutes interval:- (a) O.C.Raid and Battle H.Qrs. (b) Sub.Lieut HUNTER and Covering Party. (c) Sub.Lieut WALKER and 3 Runners. (d) "A" Raiding Party. (e) "B" do. (f) Forward Battalion H.Q. ROUTE. By Track to Dump at Q.14.d.9.4. thence to TRIGGER Avenue and QUAKER ALLEY to Q.17.c.4.4. in BEAUMONT Trench
METHOD OF ATTACK.	10.	(a) At ZERO minus 45 minutes the Raiding Party will leave the Trench at Q.17.c.4.4. and will form up along the track with their right at the junction of the track and Trench at Q.17.c.7.6. by ZERO minus 10 minutes under the supervision of the Battn Intelligence Offr. who will report the party in position by runner to O.C.Raid. (b) The barrage will open at ZERO on LUSTRE SUPPORT, LOUNGE and LOCUST Trenches. It will lift off LUSTRE SUPPORT at ZERO plus 4 mins. and off LOUNGE at ZERO plus 6 mins. When the guns shift off these trenches they will join a box barrage already formed 150 yards from the FINAL Objective.(i.e. LOUNGE Trench from Q.17.d.4.7. to Q.17.b.1.2.)

(c) At ZERO the raiding Party will close up to the barrage as near as possible, at ZERO plus 4 mins. they will rush the Trench and Crater, subsequently working along LUSTRE SUPPORT and the new trench at Q.17.central to LOUNGE Trench.

WITHDRAWAL 11.
No general signal will be given from our trenches for the withdrawal. Sub.Lieut BRIDDON (O.C. Raiding Party) will give the signal when the work is completed by a series of long blasts on the whistle, which will be repeated by all N.C.Os.

The Raiding Party will return via the old Trench running west from Q.17.central to A 7 Locality where they will be met by the Intelligence Officer and conducted to Battalion H.Qrs.

TERMINATING SIGNAL. 12.
The return of the raiding party to our trenches will be signalled by 3 Rifle Grenade Rockets which will burst into TWO RED and TWO WHITE lights also by fullerphone upon which the Artillery fire will cease. The Battn Intelligence Officer will be responsible for these signals.

NATURE OF COVERING FIRE. 13.
The Barrage on LUSTRE SUPPORT will consist of 18-pndrs, and five Stokes Mortars.

On LOUNGE and the new Trench of 18-pndrs, 4.5.Hows and 3 Stokes Mortars. The Standing and box barrage will consist of Heavy Artillery using a large proportion of H.E., Trench Mortars and Machine Guns.

Covering Fire from Artillery and Machine Guns will be placed on thr German Trenches on the opposite side of the valley in Q.17.c & d., Q.23.b., STATION ROAD Valley, and the slopes on the north east side of it.

FORWARD BATTN Headqrs. 14.
These will be established at Q.16.b.2.5. in A.4. locality by ZERO minus 1 Hour.

SYNCHRONIZATION OF WATCHES. 15.
At 7.30.p.m. on the 12th inst all Officers proceeding forward will send their watches to Battn H.Q. for adjustment to correct Brigade Time.

APPENDICES 16.
Instructions relative to dress and equipment, medical arrangements, signals etc. in connection with these orders are annexed in the form of appendices.

D.M.W.Beak
Commander R.N.V.R.
Commanding DRAKE Battalion.

Copies issued to:-
Copy No. 1   C.O.
2   O.C.Raid.
3.   Battn Intelligence Offr.
4.   O.C."A" Coy.
5.   O.C."B" "
6   O.C."C" "
7.   189th Infy Bdge.
8.   do.
9.   do.
10.   63rd (R.N.) Division.
11.   O.C.HOOD Battalion.
12.   File.
13   War Diary.
14.   Spare.

SECRET.

Appendix 'D'

"D" Coy DRAKE BATTALION OPERATION ORDER FOR RAID.

Ref. Map – 57D S.E. 1/20,000.   10th July 1918.

1. INSTRUCTIONS.

(a) Organisation of Party.

The Raiders will be divided into two parties as follows:-
I. "A" Party.- on the RIGHT, Sub.Lieut BOLT in command with P.O.BESTFORD and 25 O.Rs from 13 and 14 Platoons.
II. "B" Party.- on the LEFT, Sub.Lieut. BRIDDON in command with P.O. NETTLESHIP and 25 O.Rs from 15 & 16 platoons.

(b) Assembly.

Both "A" & "B" Parties will be lined up on Sunken Road with right of "A" Party at junction of Trench with road at Q.17.c.75.60. at ZERO minus 10 minutes.

(c) Attack.
I. ZERO.

At ZERO hour bayonets will be fixed and both "A" & "B" Parties will then crawl forward, and get close behind our own barrage.

II. ZERO plus 4 mins.

At ZERO plus 4 minutes, that is, immediately barrage lifts from LUSTRE SUPPORT (the 1st objective) the whole line will charge forward and assault LUSTRE SUPPORT. This Trench will be mopped up, special attention being given to Crater at Q.17.a.9.1. by "B" Party and to Trench junction at Q.17.d.20.75. by "A" Party.

(d) Exploiting Success.

If at discretion of Officers on the spot success is to be exploited or if no prisoners are obtained in LUSTRE SUPPORT the parties will then proceed to the 2nd Objective LOUNGE TRENCH.

(e) Method of Approach.

I. "B" Party will leave three men A.Bs WALMSLEY, ADCOCK & MARTIN at the Crater. The remainder of the party will proceed direct astride the Communication Trench over the top to LOUNGE TRENCH, both parties working in conjunction with each other. On reaching LOUNGE Trench two men A.Bs FOSTER & POWELL will take up position at junction of the two trenches. The remainder of the party will work down to the right along LOUNGE Trench until "A" Party is met.

Except L.S. SQUIRES, ABs KNOX, LOWRIE, McKENZIE & BAKER who will work up new Communication Trench to LOUNGE Trench

II. "A" Party on reaching first objective will send a party consisting of L.S.COOK, A.Bs TODD, JENKINS, JONES & KIRBY along LUSTRE SUPPORT to the right for a few yards and prevent any enemy interfering from this trench.

After "A" Party have mopped up first objective it will continue at discretion of Officer on spot to LOUNGE Trench in following manner:- L.S. COOK, A.Bs TODD, JENKINS, JONES & KIRBY will work along LUSTRE Support in trench to junction with LOUNGE Trench. All the remainder of party with the exception of A.Bs STOCKTON, SUTHERLAND & LOGAN who will stay at first Objective, will proceed over the top to the 2nd Objective, when they will work to the left and get into touch with "B" Party, mopping up all along the Trench.

After completion of mopping up both parties will return to their own Trench by the arranged route.

2.

(f) <u>Prisoners.</u> On prisoners being captured men will be detailed to take same to Raid H.Qrs in rear.

(g) <u>Signals.</u> When O.C. Raiding Party, Sub.Lieut BRIDDON, thinks that the time for withdrawing has arrived, he will blow a whistle, this signal will be taken up by all the N.C.Os. The Raiding force will then withdraw by the arranged route into our own lines reporting to Raid H.Qrs.

When the Raiding force have all returned the O.C. Raid will send up the arranged rockets, which will be three Rifle Grenade Rockets bursting into two RED and two WHITE lights to signify to Artillery and M.Gs that the raid is finished.

In addition GREEN asteroid signal Rockets (50 small stars bursting into a cone) will be sent up at 3 minutes interval, commencing at ZERO plus 10 along the Front Line Trench in order to signify to Raiding Party the direction of our own Front Line. These lights have nothing to do with the withdrawal of the parties.

W. A. Robertson.

Lieutenant R.N.V.R.
O.C. "D" Coy.
Drake Battalion.

<u>Copies issued to:-</u>

Copy No. 1. C.O.
          2. O.C.Raid.
          3. Sub.Lieut BRIDDON.
          4. Battalion Intelligence Offr.
          5. 189th Infy Brigade.
          6.   do.
          7.   do.
          8. 63rd (R.N.) Division.
          9. War Diary.
         10. File.

REPORT ON RAID CARRIED OUT BY DRAKE BATTALION ON 12th/13th JULY ON MAILLY RIGHT SECTOR.

SECTION I. **GENERAL PREPARATION FOR THE RAID.**

The first intimation that a raid was to be carried out was received on June 30th 1918 while the Battalion was holding the Advanced Forward Zone. Very active patrolling was immediately instituted in addition to the normal patrols in order to discover a suitable portion of the enemy's line to raid.

(a) <u>Reason for selection of position raided.</u>

Enemy position opposite Left of Battalion Sector was denied to us owing to Brigade on the Left carrying out a raid in this vicinity. Information was obtained by patrols that the enemy had a post in crater at Q.17.a.95.05 as Very lights were continually being sent up from this point, and our patrols always encountered machine gun fire from the same point. A post was also discovered on the Right of the Battalion Front at Q.17.d.1.1. After due consideration it was decided that the post in the crater at Q.17.a.95.05 was more suitable to raid for the following reasons :-

(1) Less wire in front of SOUTH-WEST face.
(2) It was considered that rushing the post from the SOUTH-WEST would be in the nature of a surprise as the enemy appeared to anticipate trouble from the direction of locality A.7. which is due WEST from the post. This was assumed from the fact that most of his sniping from this post was in that direction, and also the wire on the WEST and NORTH-WEST face of the post was very thick.

(b) <u>Wire cutting.</u>

Destructive shoots were carried out on the wire on the following dates :-

(1) July 5th
(2) July 10th
(3) July 11th

Battalion in the line was asked to prevent repair by the enemy of any gaps made by these shoots by keeping up short bursts of Lewis gun fire on the gaps throughout the nights.

The wire in front of the SOUTH-WEST face of the objective was mostly of the barbed concertina pattern and included both old and new wire which, (as far as could be ascertained by ground observation) appeared to be very insecurely staked to the ground. Patrol reconnaissance confirmed this.

On the 12th instant final observation of the wire showed it to be broken in many places and it was decided that further shooting should not be carried out as existing wire did not seem a big obstacle, also the raid carried out on our Right on the night of the 11th/12th would assist in making our raid the following night more of a surprise to the enemy and should wire-cutting take place on the 12th, this might tend to take away the element of surprise thus gained and place the enemy on the alert.

(c) **Patrolling.**

The two Officers of the raiding party, the Battalion I.O. and all N.C.Os of raiding parties reconnoitred the approaches to and the trenches in the vicinity of the position on four separate occasions ; In addition at least half of the men went out also to reconnoitre in small parties with N.C.Os. The remainder all viewed the objectives from our own Front Line.

(d) **Raid Practice.**

On the night of 5th/6th July the Battalion was relieved from Front Line and went into Reserve. Two models of the course, one miniature and one full size, were laid out and completed by the 7th instant. The raiding parties were first taken over the miniature course several times, and details of the trenches and also of each man's own particular job in the raid pointed out to him. The men then went over the full sized course several times as a drill in slow time, mistakes were corrected and the actual positions given to the men. They then practised several times as a "Real show" with drums and tins to simulate a barrage. A miniature of the course was then drawn on a waterproof sheet showing route out to Assembly Position, Assembly Position, trenches to be crossed, position of wire, flanks of attack, actual objectives and route to return. Each party was then lectured by its own Officer on its own particular work and positions and on the raid as a whole. They were then lectured by O.C. raid and O.C. Battalion. G.O.C., 180th Infantry Brigade talked to the men on their duties and this was followed by a further talk by G.O.C., (RN) Division on the objects of the raid and special points to be remembered. The spirit of the men was splendid and great keenness was shown throughout all the practices.

SECTION II. **GENERAL PLAN OF RAID.**

The general idea of the scheme was

(1) To assault LUSTRE SUPPORT from Q.17.d.5.7 to crater at Q.17.central paying special attention to crater which was believed to be the only portion of this first objective which was occupied by the enemy.

(2) To exploit success and clear up LOUNGE TRENCH from Q.17.d.4.7 to Q.17.d.1.9 where dugouts were believed to exist.

(a) **Method of Attack.**

It was considered that two Officers, two P.Os., and fifty O.Rs. were sufficient for the work ; they were divided equally into two parties known respectively as "A" Party and "B" Party.

(1) "A" Party of one Officer, one P.O. and 25 O.Rs. was to be responsible for the right half of the first objective, the party then to continue to known post at junction of LOUNGE TRENCH and LUSTRE SUPPORT at Q.17.d.4.7 in the following manner :- Four men working up LUSTRE SUPPORT inside trench, the remainder going astride the trench over the top. Three men of this party were to be left behind at the first objective to mop up.

(2) "B" Party of 1 Officer, 1 P.O. & 25 O.Rs to be responsible for the Left Half of the first objective, paying particular attention to the Crater at Q.17. central, party then to continue to 2nd objective in the following manner:- Four men to work up Communication Trench to LOUNGE TRENCH at Q.17.b.1.2. and the remainder of the party astride the Communication Trench over the top. Three men of this party were to be left in the Crater to mop up.

Both parties on reaching the 2nd Objective were to mop up LOUNGE Trench, "A" party working to the left and "B" party working to the right until both met when they were to return to their own front line by arranged route.

(b) **Signals.**

(i) For actual return of party by means of blasts on whistle.

(ii) In order to indicate the direction of our own front line to the raiding parties, GREEN Lights were to be sent up at pre-arranged intervals.

(iii) For barrage to cease, ROCKETS of a pre-arranged colour were to be sent up.

SECTION III. **EXECUTION OF RAID.**

On account of the muddy condition of the trenches caused by the rain of the previous day, it was considered necessary to move up to the line at ZERO minus 5 hours instead of ZERO minus 2½ hours. The raiding parties arrived in the Front Line well up to time and hot tea and meat sandwiches were issued to each raider. Punctually at ZERO minus 45 minutes after they had had a rest of an hour and a quarter in the Front Line, they started out to form up in the Assembly Position. The spacing out of the men was excellently arranged by the Officers responsible and the whole raiding party was in position at ZERO minus 15 minutes without a hitch. The barrage opened right on the second and every man automatically fixed bayonets and walked up to within 30 yards of the barrage. The line moved forward splendidly just as if they were on parade. At ZERO plus 3 minutes the party arrived at the wire which, despite a few gaps, caused some difficulty. The men persevered and won their way through the wire and charged the first objective with a lusty cheer. It was noted that the wire was loosely and sparingly staked and although a fair height it was kept down fairly easily by stepping on the centre of the concertina between the stakes.

When "B" Party on the Left arrived at the crater they found the Bosche 'standing to' and he immediately began to show opposition. Some of the Bosche were on the fire-step and some were in the trench. They refused to surrender and showed resistance, consequently they were killed. In the trench the party found 3 dugout entrances on each side ; a number of Bosche found on the steps of the entrances showed fight, they refused to come out and "P" bombs followed by Mills grenades were thrown down the entrances. It is absolutely certain that the occupants were killed. Every dugout entrance encountered, whether containing visible occupants or not, was treated in a similar manner ; one dugout was actually in flames before the party left.

The party then moved forward as arranged and then along LOUNGE TRENCH until "A" Party was met. A Bosche was found in LOUNGE TRENCH in the act of firing a light machine gun. He refused to surrender and tries to turn the gun on the party. The Officer in charge of the party killed him with his revolver and captured the gun. Another Bosche was found in the act of firing his rifle ; he was overpowered and taken prisoner and sent to Raid H.Q. making two attempts to escape on his way there. All the Bosche actually killed by this party in the trenches were searched before being left, but nothing was found on any of them, the only things found on this one prisoner were a purse and identity disc.

The Officer in charge of "B" Party continued the search but without further success and evntually withdrew his party to our lines at ZERO plus 65 minutes.

"A" Party on the Right on reaching their first objective found nothing in the trench. They then continued half right over the top to LOUNGE TRENCH ; a bombing party working up LUSTRE SUPPORT met with opposition and were bombed. The rest of the party on arriving at their second objective immediately met one Bosche, who called down a dugout and 2 or 3 others came out and surrendered. The party then worked along the trench and found 12 dugout entrances. The inmates were called upon to surrender which they did without resistance. "P" bombs were flung down all these entrances after the prisoners had come out, but on account of the number of "P" bombs failing to explode, Mills bombs were thrown down afterwards but the latter were not sufficient to burn the dugout. In this vicinity "A" Party captured altogether 21 prisoners and 1 heavy machine gun which was destroyed. The Officer in charge and 7 men of the party were responsible for the actual capture of these men. There were more Bosche in the partof the line "A" Party raided, but they were killed, and the Officer in charge returned to our own lines with his captives at ZERO plus 45 minutes.

Our Artillery and Machine Gun Support.

The barrage put up by our Artillery was excellent being exceptionally clean.

The machine gun barrage must also have been very effective if any of the enemy tried to escape over the open.

Particulars re Enemy Trenches.

The trenches were about 9 feet deep and well dug; they were in a good and fairly dry condition but no duckboards or revetments were observed. The dugouts appeared to be deep with numerous well constructed entrances. All fire positions seemed to be in small cuts into the parapet just large enough to hold one man, and in many of these small positions one rifle was seen, but none with fixed bayonets. At the crater on the Left a machine gun emplacement with several boxes of ammunition and belts was found but no gun could be seen. The wire in front of the enemy lines was fairly thick and formed a bigger obstacle than had been anticipated.

Enemy Retaliation.

At about ZERO plus 30, enemy trench mortars crumped their own Front Line including the raided area but fortunately this did not affect the progress of the raid. Most of his artillery retaliation, which commenced about ZERO plus 15 minutes appeared to be placed on the MESNIL Sector, though a few crumps came into EATON LANE.

Lights.

(a) Enemy.   Only a few lights were put up, mainly orange, with a few reds.
(b) Ours.   The GREEN asteroid lights quite failed to fulfill their purpose : instead of bursting into a great number of Green stars as expected they assumed various forms. Five out of the twelve were "duds".
   The rockets for the "Cease Barrage" signal served their purpose quite well, but three out of the seven rockets were "duds".
   The enemy lights were markedly superior to ours in every way.

Result of Raid.

Enemy Casualties.

   Prisoners   23
   Machine Guns captured   2
      (including 1 heavy gun destroyed and left in "No Mans Land").
   Enemy killed (actually seen dead)   7.
   Enemy believed killed and wounded at least 20.

Dugouts.
   18 entrances bombed and 1 dugout actually left burning.

Rifles.
   Several rifles were taken out of the enemy trenches, but owing to difficulties encountered on way back only two are now actually in our possession.

Our Own Casualties.
   Wounded.   5 O.Rs.
   Missing   1 O.R.

SECTION IV.   LESSONS LEARNED FROM RAID.

(a) For complete success it is essential that a raid be not rushed upon a Battalion but sufficient notice given to allow time for the following :-
   (i)   Active patrolling by the raiders, of the area selected for the raid.
   (ii)   Practice on a full size course.
   (iii) Opportunity of getting all the raiders together for intimate talks on the subject, illustrated by diagrams. This point is considered to be a most important one and cannot be too strongly emphasised.
   As a result of having the above privileges all reports of the raid show that each man knew his own particular job, and that the whole operation was carried out with drill-like precision.

(b) It is considered that the Officers in charge of the raiding parties, although receiving definite and detailed orders for each minute particular, should not however be tied down too strictly, in exploiting success. They should be fully trusted to use their initiative within certain bounds, and it should be made quite clear to them that upon their leadership and judgement depends the success of the operation.

(c) In the talks to the men great stress should be laid on their vast superiority man to man over the Bosche, and every effort made to work upon the men's enthusiasm.

(d) As far as we know the operation was carried out exactly as practised on the taped out course, except that one Officer and seven O.Rs. with prisoners came back by a route other than that pre-arranged.

In conclusion it is felt that the greatest credit reflects upon the two Officers and the men of the raiding parties for the grim determination which they displayed in carrying out the object of the raid.

               (sd) D.M.W. BEAK,
                    Commander, R.N.V.R.
                    Commanding Drake Battalion.

Identification Trace for use with Artillery Maps.

MAP Y

SECRET

Tracing taken from Sheet 57D S.E.
of the 1/10,000 map of
Signature

Identification Trace for use with Artillery Maps.

MAP 'Z'

Q

'D' Coy
6 Guns

'D' Coy
6 Guns

'A' Coy 8 Guns

'C' Coy
8 Guns

'B' Coy
4 Guns

'B' Coy
4 Guns

38th
4 Guns

38th Batt
4 Guns

Tracing taken from Sheet 57D SE 2

of the 1 10,000 map of

Signature

Army Form C. 2118.

DRAKE BATT WAR DIARY for August 1918.
or
INTELLIGENCE SUMMARY
(Erase heading not required.)

Vol 2

Place	Date	Hour	Summary of Events and Information	Remarks and references to Appendices
LOUVENCOURT	1st to 3rd		Company and Specialist training	ditto
PUCHEVILLERS	4th		Church parade 10.30 am – Orders to return to Puchevillers	ditto
	6th		Left LOUVENCOURT 11.30 p.m. arriving at PUCHEVILLERS 1.45 am 5th	ditto
	7th		Company and Specialist training concentrating on Lewis Guns.	ditto
	7th		Left PUCHEVILLERS 5.30 p.m. and marched to BEHENCOURT	ditto
BEHENCOURT	9th		Expecting to take part in attack on MORLANCOURT.	ditto
	11th 12th		Under an hours notice to move	ditto
	12th 13th		Practising Brigade attacks SE of village during the evenings.	ditto
SARTON	14th		Marched to SARTON in the evening receiving one hours notice to move. Arrived SARTON 2.15 am on the 15th.	ditto
	16th 17th 18th		Company field days. Two hours notice to move to VAUCHELLES. Left SARTON 8.30 evening arriving VAUCHELLES 10 pm.	ditto
VAUCHELLES	19th		Received warning order of attack within the next few days on ABLAINZEVELLE recommitted by C.O.	ditto

WAR DIARY
or
INTELLIGENCE SUMMARY
for August cont.

(Erase heading not required.)

Army Form C. 2118.

Place	Date	Hour	Summary of Events and Information	Remarks and references to Appendices
SOUASTRE	20th		Night march to SOUASTRE arriving 7.30 a.m. Conferences of Company Commanders at 7.30 a.m. & reconnaissance of BUCQUOY LINE. Battalion marched off 9.30 p.m. to Assembly position N.W. of BUCQUOY.	
	21st	ZERO. 4.55 a.m.	Battalion formed up in line of half Battalion in four at 280 yards interval & 150 yards between fronts & rear companies. "A" on left "B" on right front line. "C" Coy on left "D" on right second line. Battalion advanced in N.E. direction as far as ABLAINZEVELLE outskirts, then attacked in an easterly direction the left resting on the ABLAINZEVELLE — ACHIET-LE-GRAND road the right parallel & passing through the SOUTHERN CORNER of LOGEAST WOOD. The first line's objective was the brown line immediately EAST of the WOOD. The second line C & D to form through & occupy the	

Army Form C. 2118.

WAR DIARY
or
INTELLIGENCE SUMMARY
(Erase heading not required.)

Instructions regarding War Diaries and Intelligence Summaries are contained in F.S. Regs., Part II. and the Staff Manual respectively. Title Pages will be prepared in manuscript.

Place	Date	Hour	Summary of Events and Information	Remarks and references to Appendices
	21st Cont'd		BAPAUME - ARRAS - ALBERT RAILWAY. A + B Companies to follow up in support. HOODS & HAWKES on our right 188th Brigade on our left.	
			The attack met little resistance until reaching LOBEAST WOOD when Machine Guns opened fire but were quickly overcome. B Company advanced through the wood A + C down the road & D Company covered the southern edge of the wood. A + B Company early gained their objectives & C + D reached ACHIET-LE-GRAND - ACHIET LE PETIT ROAD but had to retire 200 yards owing to no one being in touch on the left. They consolidated this line and held up a counter attack.	
	22nd		Carried on consolidation & helped greatly in breaking up counter-attack against MARINES and IRISH on our left. Relieved by 37th Division at 2am 23rd. Casualties Killed - 3 Off. 26 OR. Wounded. 3 " 86 " Missing etc. 49	

2449 Wt. W14957/Mgo 750,000 1/16 J.B.C. & A. Forms/C.2118/12.

WAR DIARY or INTELLIGENCE SUMMARY

Army Form C. 2118.

Place	Date	Hour	Summary of Events and Information	Remarks and references to Appendices
BUCQUOY.	23rd		Settled down in the British support line	
	24th	2.30 am	orders to clear EAST of BUCQUOY by 6 am.	
		12.30 am	moved to ACHIET-LE-PETIT. Tea - assembled on high ground between ACHIET-LE-PETIT & LOPART WOOD. Enemy aeroplanes attacked Brigade with Machine Guns and Bombs. No casualties to Drakes. - ATTACK on LEBARQUE at 7.30 p.m. cancelled.	
	25th	ZERO 5 am.	attacked through LOPART WOOD. A Company advanced & overran enemy line SE of WOOD & HAMNE BATTn passed through followed by "C" & D Company's in column. J found at 100 yards interval and A & B in rear. Brigade held up by strong point expect C & D who shewed round to the NORTH and reached LE BARQUE VILLAGE and the high ground to the south. HOOD Battalion reinforced front and captured strong point & then Brigade	

WAR DIARY or INTELLIGENCE SUMMARY

Army Form C. 2118.

Place	Date	Hour	Summary of Events and Information	Remarks and references to Appendices
	25/26 26th 27th		proceeded & consolidated on ridge SOUTH of LE BARQUE BRIGADE reorganised. HAWKE on right, HOOD in centre & DRAKE on left. 21st Division on the night on 187th on the left occupying the village. German counter attack on left flank of Hawke shell fire during the whole time also Heavy gun fire during the morning of the 27th. 21st Division adv[anced] and relieved us at 12 midnight. Casualties Killed 2 offr 5 ORs Wounded 2 offr 60 " Missing 2 "	
	28th 29th		Battalion returned to MIRAUMONT. Time spent in cleaning up.	
	30th		Orders to move to BOIRY-ST-RICTRUDE. Marched off 10.30 pm arriving 2.30 am 31st	
	31st		Formed camp, fetching tents and bivouac sheets.	

D.M.b. Beak
Commander RNVR
Commanding DRAKE BATTN

"DRAKE" Bn
War Diary
Sepr. 1918

WAR DIARY
or
INTELLIGENCE SUMMARY.

Place	Date	Hour	Summary of Events and Information	Remarks and references to Appendices
BOIRY ST. RICTRUDE	1/9/18		Preparation for move. Carried out, passed ASSTT Point at 7 p.m. and spent the night in trenches at T.4.d (SHEET.51.6)	
	2/9/18		at 4 A.M. we moved through FONTAINE-LEZ-CROISILLES and HENDECOURT passing through the 57 DIV, we moved through CAGNICOURT, and on to the BOIS-DE-BOUCHS frozen than (?) the 188BDE at 4 pm, The Bn attacked Railway Line Lyn (?) 1570 yds in front of west and succeeded in overrunning all opposition, the Bn pushed on for a further 2500 yds either side the INCHY-PROVILLE Rd Capturing the HINDENBURG SUPPORT LINE, this was completed by 8 pm	
	3.		The Bn mopped up the Hindenburg Line and pushed on to TADPOLE COPSE which was consolidated by 4 pm	
	4.		At 9.30 AM The Bn swept down through MOEUVRES but was severely enveloped. Heavy shell fire was forced to withdraw to the HINDENBURG SUPPORT Line in Rear of the village	
	5		At 9 AM Relief Completed by 7. R.F.s. (190BDE) and we moved back to V14. (Sheet 51.G)	

"DRAKE" Bn.
War Diary
Sept 1918.

Army Form C. 2118.

WAR DIARY
or
INTELLIGENCE SUMMARY.

(Erase heading not required.)

Place	Date	Hour	Summary of Events and Information	Remarks and references to Appendices
	6		Moved to HINDENBERG Line at QUEANT - very QUIET	JMP
	7		Relieved by 2/4 LOYAL N. LANCS 57th Div by 2pm and marched to point on the CROISILLES-FONTAINE Road.	JMP
	8		Bn Entrained at BOYELLE and detrained at LA HERIÈRE and marched to BARLY which was reached at 12.30 AM on 9th	JMP
BARLY	9		Reorganisation	JMP
"	10		Reorganisation	JMP
"	11			
"	12		TRaining	JMP
"	13			
"	14			
"	15		Church Parade	JMP
"	16		Training	JMP
RANSART	17		Bn moved forward to RANSART	JMP
"	18		Bde Scheme to ST LEGER	JMP
ST LEGER	19		Training	JMP
"	20		Training	JMP
"	21		Training	JMP
"	22		Church Parade	JMP

WAR DIARY
or
INTELLIGENCE SUMMARY.

Army Form C. 2118.

DRAKE Bn
War Diary
Sept 1918.

Place	Date	Hour	Summary of Events and Information	Remarks and references to Appendices
ST LEGER	23		Training	
	24		Training	
	25		At 6 pm Bn moved to Sunken Rd S. of Pronville which was reached at 10.30 pm	
PRONVILLE	26		Bn lay under cover all day	
	27		At 1.30 am Bn moved to assembly position S. of MOEUVRES and were in position by 3.30 am & at 5.20 am the 190 d attacked the CANAL-DU-NORD under a great Barrage. the Bn passed through the 1BdeBde which were holding in Rear of ANNEUX and GRAINCOURT. During which we passed through ? Rd ft of the FACTORY and through the Railway bridge of GRAINCOURT to KNAVE TRENCH where we were Relieved by the 57 Bn Westward to the FACTORY for the night.	
MOEUVRES	28		At 9 am Bn moved forward through the 57 Bn at 4 pm and attacked the L'ESCAULT CANAL and succeeded in getting a few across same, under cover of Darkness the Bn returned the CANAL and Established 3 posts across the River.	
	29		Progress across the River was a freed by 12.30 pm and enemy Retired through the MARCOING LINE to the EAST of the BOIS-DE-PARIS, Bn were relieved and came back to LA MANIERE for the night	
	30		At 7.30 am Bn again moved forward to the Road East of BOIS DE-PARIS but were again cleared and went back to LA MANIERE by 9.20 pm	

Cattermillar
Capt

D W C RNE
ac E RNR
GRAKE Bn

KILLED 3
WOUNDED 42
MISSING —
TOTAL 45

6 officers
Men

KILLED 11
WOUNDED 302
MISSING 25
TOTAL 384

Army Form C. 2118.

WAR DIARY
or
INTELLIGENCE SUMMARY.
(Erase heading not required.)

Drake Bn.   Vol 28

Place	Date	Hour	Summary of Events and Information	Remarks and references to Appendices
	1/10/18.		Battalion relieved by H.L.I.(52nd Divn) at 16.00 hours.	
	2/10/18.		Battalion moved back to Wally S. of ANNEUX.	
	3/10/18.		Reorganisation of Coys. Moved at 18.00 hours to Sunken road N.E. of GRAINCOURT.	
	5/10/18.		Reorganisation and training.	
	6/10/18.		Moved up to NOYELLES at 18.45 hours.	
	7/10/18.		In assembly trenches at RUMILLY by 03.45 hours. Jumped off at 04.30 and gained objective by 07.00 hours, which was 100 yards W. of NIERGNIES. Counter attack by Bosche on HOOD Battalion held up on our consolidated line when the HOOD Battalion fell back to that point at 09.30.	
	8/10/18.		Battalion relieved when two battalions of the 24th Divn. had passed through at 10.30 hours. Arrived at old billets at GRAINCOURT at 01.00 hours. At 10.00 hours Battalion marched back to MORCHIES.	
	9/10/18.		Reorganising.	
	10/10/18.		Battalion entrained at VAULX VRAUCOURT, at 14.15 hours and detrained at PETIT HOUVIN at 23.00 hours. Marched into BUNNEVILLE at Midnight.	
	11/10/18.		Reorganisation and kit inspection.	
	12/10/18.		Church Parade.	
	13/10/18.		Training.	
	14/10/18.		Battalion moved to LINGUEREUIL.	
	20/10/18.		Training.	
	21/10/18.			
	22/10/18.			
	31/10/18.			

Sub.Lieut. R.N.V.R.,
A/Adjt. DRAKE Battalion.
for O.C. DRAKE BN.

Army Form C. 2118.

WAR DIARY
or
INTELLIGENCE SUMMARY
(Erase heading not required.)

Instructions regarding War Diaries and Intelligence Summaries are contained in F. S. Regs., Part II. and the Staff Manual respectively. Title Pages will be prepared in manuscript.

Drake Bn
Vol 30

Place	Date	Hour	Summary of Events and Information	Remarks and references to Appendices
	1918 Nov.1.		Battalion embussed at LEIN COURT and arrived at AUBY at 16.00 hours.	
	Nov 2nd & 3rd.		Training.	
	Nov.4th		Battalion embussed at AUBY and debussed at DOUCHY at 15.00 hours.	
	Nov.5th.		Marched to AULNOY.	
	Nov.6th.		Marched to SEBOURQUIAUX	
	Nov.7th.		Brigade attacked from ANGRE. Battalion passed through the HOOD Battalion at AUDREGNIES and pushed on to the outskirts of village of WIHERIES in T.20.b, T.21.a. and T.15.c. & d., Sheet 45. In touch with 4th Canadian Division on left of HOOD Battalion on right.	
	Nov 8th.		Battalion attacked WIHERIES at 08.00 hours and passed through to final position in T.24.a. & c. Sheet 45. Battalion billeted in WIHERIES for the night.	
	Nov.9th.		Battalion moved to LA HAUT.DIT. PETIT-DOUR.	
	Nov.10th.		Battalion moved to SARS-LA-BRUYERE and thence to QUEVY-LE-PETIT.	
	Nov.11th.		Battalion in support to HAWKE and HOOD Battalions and moved forward at 09.30 hours. ARMISTICE came into force at 11.00 hours. Battalion reached GIVRY.	
	No.12th & 13th.		Reorganisation.	
	Nov.14th to 26th.		Training.	
	Nov.27th.		Battalion moved to LE CAMP PERDU.	

Army Form C. 2118.

WAR DIARY
or
INTELLIGENCE SUMMARY

(Erase heading not required.)

Place	Date	Hour	Summary of Events and Information	Remarks and references to Appendices
	Nov.28th. to 30th.		Training.	
			CASUALTIES.	
			Killed. Wounded. Missing. Total.	
			Officers. — 2 — 2	
			Men. 5 53 1 59	
			GRAND TOTAL. 61	

J. Maxwell
Sub.Lieut. R.N.V.R.
I.O., DRAKE Battalion.

Army Form C. 2118.

WAR DIARY
or
INTELLIGENCE SUMMARY.

(Erase heading not required.)

DRAKE Bn

Place	Date	Hour	Summary of Events and Information	Remarks and references to Appendices
DOUR	1/12/18		Church Parade	
	2		Military Training	
	3		Rehearsal Parade for Corps Commanders Inspection	
	4		Military Training	
	5		— do —	
	6		— do —	
	7		— do —	
	8		Church Parade	
	9		Military and Educational Training	
	10		— do —	
	11		Route march with 1st Line Transport	
	12		Military + Educational Training	
	13		— do —	
	14		— do —	
	15		Church Parade	
	16		Military and Educational Training	
	17		— do —	
	18		Classifying Examination of all men undergoing Elem Education	
	19		Route march	
	20		Military + Educational Training	

WAR DIARY
or
INTELLIGENCE SUMMARY.

Army Form C. 2118.

Place	Date	Hour	Summary of Events and Information	Remarks and references to Appendices
DOUR	21/12/19		Military + Educational Training	
"	22		Church Parade	
"	23		Military Educational Training	
"	24		— do —	— do —
"	25		Church Parade	
"	26		Inspection Parade	
"	27		Route March	
"	28		Military Educational Training	
"	29		— do —	— do —
"	30		— do —	— do —
"	31		— do —	— do —

J. Clarke. Lt. R.N.V.R.
for
O.C. "DRAKE" Bn

Army Form C. 2118.

WAR DIARY
or
INTELLIGENCE SUMMARY.
(Erase heading not required.)

Drake

Place	Date	Hour	Summary of Events and Information	Remarks and references to Appendices
DOUR	From 1st January 1919. to 31st January 1919.		During the month of January 1919 the Battalion was stationed at DOUR, BELGIUM. This period was devoted to Military Training, Education, Sports and Demobilisation. Casualties:- NIL. Demobilised during the month:- 3 Officers and 246 O.Rs. 1/2/19. D.M.S. Reak Commander R.N.V.R., Commanding DRAKE Battalion.	

Army Form C. 2118.

WAR DIARY
or
INTELLIGENCE SUMMARY.
(Erase heading not required.)

Instructions regarding War Diaries and Intelligence Summaries are contained in F.S. Regs., Part II. and the Staff Manual respectively. Title pages will be prepared in manuscript.

WO 32

Place	Date	Hour	Summary of Events and Information	Remarks and references to Appendices
DOUR, BELGIUM.	1919 Feb.		Month of February 1919 devoted to Battalion Training, Educational Training, Sports, and Demobilisation.	
	21/2/19.		Battalion presented with the King's Colours by General Sir H.S.Horne, K.C.B., K.C.M.G., Commanding First Army, at Dour in Belgium at 11.00 hours. Senior Major:- Lieut O.A.Heath M.C., R.N.V.R. Senior Subaltern:- Sub Lieut J.K.MacLean, R.N.V.R. Casualties:- Nil. Demobilised during month: - 1 Officer and 218 O.Rs.	

D. b. Peak
Commander, R.N.V.R.
Commanding DRAKE Battalion.

Army Form C. 2118.

WAR DIARY
or
INTELLIGENCE SUMMARY.

(Erase heading not required.)

WO 33

Place	Date	Hour	Summary of Events and Information	Remarks and references to Appendices

LOUR, Belgium.	1919 March		Month of March 1919 devoted to Battalion Training, Educational Training, Sports, and Demobilisation.
			
			Casualties:- NIL.
			
			Demobilised during month:- 11 Officers and 141 O.Rs.
			
			                                                  Lieut Commander, R.N.V.R.,
			                                                  Commanding Drake Battalion.	

Instructions regarding War Diaries and Intelligence Summaries are contained in F. S. Regs., Part II. and the Staff Manual respectively. Title pages will be prepared in manuscript.

Army Form C. 2118.

Drake Bn

WAR DIARY
or
INTELLIGENCE SUMMARY.

(Erase heading not required.)

Instructions regarding War Diaries and Intelligence Summaries are contained in F.S. Regs., Part II. and the Staff Manual respectively. Title pages will be prepared in manuscript.

Place	Date	Hour	Summary of Events and Information	Remarks and references to Appendices
Lour, Belgium.	1919 April.		Month of April 1919 devoted to Battalion sports and Demobilisation. Casualties:- Nil. Demobilised during the month:- 16 Officers and 81 O.Rs.	

D.E.A. Pick
Commander R.N.V.R.,
Commanding Drake Battalion.

www.ingramcontent.com/pod-product-compliance
Lightning Source LLC
Chambersburg PA
CBHW051526190426
43193CB00045BA/2073